'We cannot escape history.'
President Abraham Lincoln

*'We shall all be judged by history . . .
and I shall write the history.'*
Winston Churchill

'All history teaches . . .'
Anon.

'History is written by the winners.'
George Orwell

*'Let us learn our lessons. Never, never, never
believe any war will be smooth or easy, or that
anyone who embarks on the strange voyage can
measure the tides and hurricanes he will
encounter. The statesman who yields to war
fever must realize that once the signal is given,
he is no longer master of policy but the slave of
unforeseeable and uncontrollable events.'*
Winston Churchill

*'History is a story, a story needs a narrator and
a narrator needs to be standing somewhere. a
view from nowhere does not work.'*
Tony Judt

The HAND *of* HISTORY

The HAND *of* HISTORY

An Anthology of History Quotations and Commentaries

Edited by
Michael Leventhal

Illustrated by
Chris Riddell

Greenhill Books, Elstree

Robin Brass Studio, Montreal

Jonathan Ball Publishers, Johannesburg & Cape Town

The Hand of History
This edition published in 2011 by Greenhill Books,
3 Barham Avenue, Elstree, Herts, WD6 3PW
www.greenhillbooks.com

Greenhill Books are distributed by Pen & Sword Books Ltd,
47 Church Street, Barnsley, S. Yorkshire, S70 2AS, England

Published in Canada in 2011 by Robin Brass Studio Inc.
www.rbstudiobooks.com

ISBN: 978-1-84832-623-1

CIP data records for this title are available
from the British Library

Library and Archives Canada Cataloguing in Publication
The hand of history : an anthology of quotes and commentaries / edited by
Michael Leventhal ; drawings by Chris Riddell.

Includes bibliographical references.
Co-published by: Greenhill Books.
ISBN 978-1-84832-623-1

1. World history – Quotations, maxims, etc.
I. Leventhal, Michael E. J.

D20.H35 2011   909   C2011-903721-1

Printed in Great Britain by CPI Mackays, Chatham

Typeset in 9.5/11.5 point Minion Pro

Contents

Introduction

The title for this book was taken from Tony Blair's remark on the eve of Northern Ireland's Good Friday Agreement. On 8 April 1998, the then prime minister declared, 'A day like today is not a day for soundbites, we can leave those at home. But I feel the hand of history upon our shoulder . . . I really do.' In an era renowned in Britain for political spin, the leader of the Labour Party professed to disparage soundbites and yet in the same breath he delivered the most memorable one of his career.

Blair's comment seems an apt starting-point: aside from being a wonderful piece of irony it provides a typical example of how history is authoritatively invoked by world leaders. The resolution of a relatively small matter is pronounced 'historic' to inflate the importance of the event and usually the ego of the leader too. History is presented as an omniscient authority that provides a true reckoning – normally one that chimes with the speaker's version of events.

For centuries, politicians and commentators have employed historical precedents to justify political and military strategies. But history can easily be abused; besides simple falsification a selective use of historical facts can be equally misleading. When intellectuals and politicians from nascent or would-be states speak of constructing a 'national identity' or a 'national history' it invariably entails a parade of partisan facts to support a particular narrative. That said, all history is necessarily selective. Moreover, people have varying perceptions of the history they share. Those differences are often the source of misunderstanding and conflict.

My aim in preparing this anthology was to delve into some of these issues. A number of leading historians were invited either to write an aphorism about history or to select a quote about history or its writing. They were also asked to provide a short commentary explaining their choice. More than one hundred historians worldwide responded and the result is a remarkable roll-call of the most respected writers on history today. I worried that their commentaries might be repetitious. Far from it. A welcome aspect of this collection is the diversity of their responses.

One theme that has emerged is the changing role of the individual in the writing of history. This tallies with my experience as a reader and a publisher: in recent decades there has been an increasing emphasis on both the role of the ordinary individual and also the details of their lives. It is what might be termed the 'personalization of history'. Arguably it has come at the expense of grand sweeping narratives in all schools of history.

Traditional Marxist histories have concentrated on movements of impersonal power and underlying forces rather than particular individuals. But then, in 1963, E. P. Thompson published his seminal social history, *The Making of the English Working Class*. Thompson announced his intention to 'rescue the poor stockinger, the Luddite cropper, the "obsolete" hand-loom weaver . . . from the enormous condescension of posterity'.

A similar, significant point for military readers – my own discipline – was John Keegan's *Face of Battle*, published more than a decade later in 1976. The author explicitly stated that his intention was to move from the grandiose canvases of military history and to focus instead on the minutiae of individual lives. And Keegan was right: people like to read about people.

Neither Keegan nor Thompson was simply pandering to the market but they both appreciated that readers had started to want life injected into high politics and strategy. They want to understand how people – and not just kings and commanders – ate, slept, danced and died. In this context, the success of Max Arthur's recent *Voices* series – compilations of twentieth-century personal accounts – is not surprising: eyewitness testimonies can provide the most vivid, basic and emotive picture of individual lives in the past.

This personalisation is one reason that history, particularly narrative history, now appeals to much wider audiences; Peter Furtado, for ten years the editor of *History Today* magazine, suggested to me that the sale of history books is greater than ever because 'the "story" has been put back into "history"'.

This significant change has coincided with – and has partly been a product of – the general democratization of Western society from the 1960s and 1970s. With the erosion of class barriers and a decline of deference to authority, readers have expected more equality in the subjects of history.

I was recently fortunate to publish *Secret Days*, the Bletchley Park account of Asa Briggs. Lord Briggs, ninety this year, described his journey from economic historian in the 1940s, to social historian, cultural historian, and finally 'human historian' with the publication of his wartime experiences, in which he was writing as both an historian and a former participant. He conceded that his personal development may have been the result of a disdain for the institutionalization of 'sub-histories' but it also reflects his reactions to the changes that have taken place in the writing of history during the past seventy years.

These developments may be a consequence of the growth in the range of media in which history can be presented. History is more accessible than ever before; it appears in prime-time documentaries on television every night and it can be found online at all times. And thanks to the internet anyone with a pinch of curiosity can conduct their own researches into their genealogy or any aspect of history in almost any language. Access to materials online did not engender the rise of interest in family history but it has made such investigations easier and more appealing.

The progress of technology has led to what Arnold Toynbee described as the 'annihilation of distance'. Toynbee made this statement in 1952 and since then the pace of that change has only increased. Today, writers around the world can publish, promote and discuss their work online within minutes. This has helped break down 'silos'; ideas and information move so quickly between genres and disciplines that it can lead to original cross-fertilization. It has also significantly broadened the scope of history writing.

This evolution and expansion will continue and trends will emerge; the style of history writing will develop, as will the expectations and demands of readers. Perhaps we are already seeing the start of a shift back towards the grand narrative. The success of authors such as Niall Ferguson and Andrew Roberts suggests that there is still a healthy appetite for the latter genre. But across all genres there has been an important change: even 'broad-brush' histories now contain more of the 'human touch'. It has become an essential ingredient of history writing.

*

I owe a great debt to the historians who have supported this venture which is raising money for Parkinson's research. Among the contributors was the late Richard Holmes, whose piece reached me very recently. In addition to the writers, Chris Riddell has provided brilliant illustrations. I am grateful to Donald Sommerville, my long-suffering editor; Shona Andrew, who designed the book jacket; friends who were good enough to proof-read the work and make suggestions; and Jem Butcher, who designed the end-papers. Finally I owe thanks to my father, who taught me everything I know about the world of publishing.

Michael Leventhal,
August 2011
michael@frontline-books.com

CHARLES ALLEN

'What the learned world demands of us in India is to be quite certain of our data, to place the monumental record before them exactly as it now exists, and to interpret it faithfully and literally.'

James Prinsep

The words were written by James Prinsep, Secretary of the Asiatic Society of Bengal, in 1837 at the onset of the illness that led to his death a year later. Over the previous months 37-year-old Prinsep had published a series of *coups d'érudition* that included the unravelling of the Brahmi and Kharosthi alphabets, thereby allowing him to read the mysterious pillar and rock edicts scattered across the land that had baffled scholars for centuries. That led in turn to the revelation of their author as Ashoka, first and arguably greatest of India's emperors.

Few scholars have come close to matching Prinsep's achievements, few have suffered such neglect. Prinsep regarded himself as a scientist, but he was by definition an Orientalist, therefore tainted as part of the exploitative machinery of European imperialism. No matter that he and his fellow Orientalists had led the fight against the Macauleyites and Evangelicals who called for the imposition of English values and English education on India.

Today it is Ashoka who is under a cloud. When India achieved independence in 1947 he was all the rage. To symbolise the new secular India Prime Minister Nehru selected an Ashokan image, the 24-spoked wheel known as the *chakra*, to be set at the centre of the Indian tricolour. The Ashoka boom ended with the assassination of Nehru's daughter, Prime Minister Indira Gandhi, in 1984 and the rise of sectarian political parties whose rallying-cry was *Hindutva* or 'Hinduness'. One of the victims of *Hindutva* has been India's leading Ashoka scholar, Professor Romila Thapar, whose reading of the history of India as set down in the national school syllabus was altered in what she saw as 'an attempt to replace mainstream history with a *Hindutva* version of history'. Thapar's protests led to her being accused of betraying India, a double irony in that the emperor she wrote about was himself a victim of *Hindutva* in one of its earliest manifestations.

Hindutva has no time for the religious tolerance that Emperor Ashoka called for in his Seventh Rock Edict, where he spoke of his desire 'that all religions should reside everywhere'. It has no time for history based on facts.

Prinsep's words continue to resonate.

JOYCE APPLEBY

'The value of history is not scientific but moral.
By liberalizing the mind, by deepening the sympathies,
by fortifying the will, history enables us to control not
society, but ourselves – a much more important thing;
it prepares us to live more humanely in the present
and to meet rather than to foretell the future.'

Carl Becker

I have quoted this line from Becker many times because it expresses so perfectly what the study of history can yield. Unlike science, people can benefit from history only by making it their personal possession and thinking deeply about its meaning. Becker's line describes a role for history that is both modest and profound.

RICK ATKINSON

'History, like tragedy, requires an exposition, a central action, and a dénouement. My secret is to force the reader to wonder: Will Philip V ascend the throne?'

Voltaire

There is great utility in borrowing from the other arts, and perhaps you'll pardon my reckless ambition in borrowing from Voltaire when I say: 'My secret is to encourage the reader to wonder: Will the Allies win the Second World War?'

And Jacques Barzun, the philosopher and writer who is now 102 years old, demands that historical narrative accommodate what he describes as 'the range and wildness of individuality, the pivotal force of trifles, the manifestations of greatness, [and] the failures of unquestioned talent'. As a writer of narrative military history, I can only wonder: Was ever there a more succinct description of men at war?

JULIET BARKER

'If one could make alive again for other people some cobwebbed skein of old dead intrigues and breathe breath and character into dead names and stiff portraits. That is history to me.'

G. M. Trevelyan

Biographies, we are told, are out of fashion. Yet for me people have always been at the heart of history. Lessons at school were dull and boring: a worthy trudge through politics, economics, social trends, none of which captured my imagination in the same way as the historical fiction I read avidly at home. Walter Scott, Nigel Tranter, Margaret Irwin, Norah Lofts conjured up characters from the past and told a story about them with which one could empathise and therefore understand. They brought history to life by seeing it from the individual's point of view – and that is something I have tried to do in my own writing.

People's lives may be shaped by events but individual people also shape those events. Agincourt is a classic example. There would have been no campaign, and indeed no victory, had it not been for one man: Henry V. It was his ambition, his meticulous attention to logistical detail, his tactical skill and, at the crucial moment on the battlefield, his ability to inspire his men with his personal bravery and charisma in the face of overwhelming odds, which won the day.

Yet there might have been no battle at all had it not been for another man, a French knight now almost completely forgotten even in his own country. Raoul de Gaucourt brought 300 reinforcements into Harfleur under Henry's nose and defended the town for so long that the King was forced to abandon his plans for further conquest and seek battle instead. (Gaucourt spent ten years in an English prison for his pains but dedicated the rest of his life to fighting the English; astonishingly, he lived to see them driven out of France in 1453.)

There is an even greater thrill in unearthing other forgotten individuals who would never normally earn a place in the history books at all: the English esquire forced to pawn his possessions because he ran out of money when the expedition was delayed; two Welshmen who, after Agincourt, made a pilgrimage 'in fulfilment of vows made on the battlefield'; the Frenchwoman who, six months after the battle, did not know whether she was a wife or a widow because her husband's body could not be found. It is stories like these that, for me, breathe life and character not only into dead names but also into history itself.

CORRELLI BARNETT

Uxbridge: 'My Lord, I have lost my leg.'
Wellington: 'By God, so you have!'

This conversation on horseback took place in the midst of the Battle of Waterloo between His Grace Field Marshal the Duke of Wellington and his second-in-command, the Earl of Uxbridge, after Uxbridge had been struck by a cannonball.

To me this is a superb example of traditional English self-control and understatement, which should serve as an antidote to all the facile emoting indulged in today by politicians, theatrical 'luvvies', and vox-pops interviewed on television.

The Duke's cool nerve and tactical judgement under fire were responsible for Bonaparte's utter defeat at Waterloo, and so shaped the future of Europe. His victory also demonstrates that at decisive moments, history is made by individuals rather than by Marxist mass movements.

MARY BEARD

'Until lions have their historians, tales of the hunt shall always glorify the hunter.'

Nigerian proverb

I am very fond of this proverb for its nice insistence that we should always remember that history has more than one side.

That's particularly important to me, as a historian of the ancient world, because almost all my evidence comes from the side of the hunters: the men (not the women), the free (not the slaves), the rich (not the poor), the Greeks and Romans (not the barbarians), the victorious (not the defeated – though, to be fair, there are rather more of these than of the other categories).

If nothing else, the idea of the 'historian of the lions' prompts me to overturn some of the standard language of historical description that can seem so neutral, but in truth never is. Instead of saying 'The Romans won another tremendous victory', try saying 'The Romans were guilty of another tremendous massacre'. It makes a big difference to the story that you tell.

When I am teaching my students, I use this proverb to undermine the idea of 'objective' history. It's all too easy to think that bias in history is bad, and that objectivity is good. But objectivity is usually a euphemism for the history of the victors, or the history of the hunters. What, I ask them, would an objective history of the Iraq War look like? Would we want it even if we could have it? And what might that tell us about an objective history of (say) Boudicca's rebellion in Britain?

I don't know where exactly this proverb comes from, or when. That, after all, is part of the point of proverbs. You can't easily pin them down. But the fact that it comes from Africa gives it another, even sharper, edge. For we Europeans, until relatively recently, would comfortably say that Africa had no history until we came along.

Quite how wrong were we? Very wrong. But that is another story.

ANTONY BEEVOR

*'The only thing we learn from history is that
nobody learns from history.'*

Otto von Bismarck

I would choose Bismarck's dictum because this remark, although a rather
cynical exaggeration, is particularly relevant now.

The real danger of historical ignorance comes from politicians making
false parallels with earlier major events. In the past decade we have seen

George W. Bush compare the 11 September attack on the United States to Pearl Harbor. Whether or not he was trying to assume the mantle of a great wartime leader, it encouraged him to follow and try to justify a state-on-state strategy rather than treat the threat as a security problem.

The Second World War has become a compulsive reference point. Eden obsessively compared Nasser to Hitler and blundered into the Suez fiasco. Rumsfeld's acolytes tried to depict Saddam Hussein as a Hitler when, if anything, he was a poor man's Stalin. They also predicted that the defeated Iraqis would cooperate with their occupiers afterwards, just like the Germans and the Japanese after 1945.

All the old jibes about generals trying to fight the next war with the tactics of the last are misplaced. It is politicians who try to justify military intervention, using the outdated rhetoric of the Second World War, simply because of its iconic status as the fight that was right.

MARTIN BELL

In some two dozen countries, from Cambodia to Angola and from Croatia to Iraq, the most important subject to study is land mine awareness. For the rest of us it is history. If we ignore it, we are indeed doomed to repeat it. There is not a regiment in the British Army, or even a predecessor regiment of today's merged regiments, that does not have Afghanistan or Mesopotamia (Iraq) on its colours. And where were our soldiers deployed most recently? In Iraq and Afghanistan. Like the Balkans, they produced more history than they could consume locally. If we do not understand our history it will ambush us, over and over again. We cannot afford a future like our past. Nor can we afford to have matters of life and death decided any longer in a Government and Parliament which are history-free zones.

ALAN BENNETT

My only quotation would be Rudge's remark in *The History Boys* – 'History is just one fucking thing after another'. Said originally, I think, by Sir Herbert Butterfield as either 'one bloody thing after another' or 'one damned thing after another'.

CONRAD BLACK

'From the sublime to the ridiculous is a single step.'

Napoleon Bonaparte

This remark was uttered just as Napoleon began the retreat from Moscow, and while he may not have foreseen the proportions of the debacle about to ensue, he certainly realized that a colossal defeat was in train. To retain such composure and such a sense of irony in such circumstances requires a mind that never loses awareness of the dramatic character of even severe adversity, and is philosophical about the fluctuations of fortune even on a gigantic scale and at an intensely personal level. And, of course, it is a very applicable comment. Who could have imagined that after rising to overwhelming military and economic power and popular cultural influence and moral authority in two long lifetimes, and then disposing of a mortal adversary in a 45-year, relatively bloodless containment policy, to emerge as the world's only great power, the United States would outsource millions of low-skill jobs while importing millions of low-skilled workers, would borrow trillions from China and Japan to buy the goods that had been outsourced from China and Japan, and would force the private and quasi-private sectors to issue trillions of dollars of worthless real-estate based securities?

That country's position was sublime as the Berlin Wall came down, and was ridiculous when George W. Bush said, with less than Rooseveltian eloquence, of the USA's $14 trillion economy: 'The sucker could go down.' In the life of a great nation, it was a single step.

JEREMY BLACK

'The evening sun seemed to linger to gild the victorious standard of Austria.'

Prince Eugene of Savoy

Much makes an impression, but to offer a lasting impression it is necessary to think back to quotations or passages of reading decades ago that have lasted in the memory. Prince Eugene's report from his dramatic and total victory over the Ottoman Turks at Zenta in Hungary in 1697 struck home because of the poetic image. The idea of the natural world deferring to that of man is ridiculous but magnificent. Zenta was not only a great victory but a key triumph in the making of a new Europe, one that was not under the sway of non-Christian powers. As such Zenta prepared the way for Edward Gibbon's confidence in *Decline and Fall* (1776–88) that the 'barbarian' invasions could not triumph anew.

The reality of battle is grim, but Eugene's report captured another reality of noble human endeavour.

GEOFFREY BLAINEY

'Distance is as characteristic of Australia as mountains are of Switzerland. By sealanes or airlanes most parts of Australia are at least 12,000 miles from western Europe, the source of most of their people, equipment, institutions and ideas. The coastline of Australia also stretches for 12,000 miles.'

'In the eighteenth century the world was becoming one world but Australia was still a world of its own. It was untouched by Europe's customs and commerce. It was more isolated than the Himalayas or the heart of Siberia.'

These two quotations come from my book, *The Tyranny of Distance: How Distance Shaped Australia's History.* The book understandably created controversy because it tried to rewrite much of Australia's history. Some of that new version of history is now accepted; some is not. Meanwhile the phrase coined by the book became part of the Australian language and then began to travel overseas.

By the 1990s the astonishing shrinking of the world challenged the very idea of 'the tyranny of distance'. Rupert Murdoch in speeches and Frances Cairncross in her 1997 London book, *The Death of Distance*, after noting my arguments, persuasively pointed out that new communications were reshaping the globe. In the 2001 edition of my book I accepted several of their themes but explained in some detail that others did not fit Australia and comparable lands. My conclusion was: 'Distance is tamed but far from dead.'

Geography is so pervasive in history that this kind of debate will not go away.

MICHAEL BLISS

'Isn't that unspeakably wonderful?'
Elizabeth Hughes

'Isn't that unspeakably wonderful?' exclaimed fifteen-year-old Elizabeth Hughes to her mother in 1922. Elizabeth was describing the effects on her body of injections of insulin, just discovered at the University of Toronto as a therapy for diabetes mellitus. Elizabeth, one of the first to receive the new substance, had been reduced to 45 pounds by her diabetes and was within days of dying when she began getting insulin that August. Within six months she had more than doubled in weight, returned to her family, and began living a normal life. In 1980, fifty-eight years later, I interviewed Elizabeth Hughes for my book, *The Discovery of Insulin*.

We are taught to shun judgements about history as a record of progress. Surely there are exceptions. Our triumphs over disease and suffering – from vaccination through insulin through antibiotics through transplants through joint replacement and so much more – are inspiring examples of modern medicine's ability to alter the human condition for the better. Very few people alive today would prefer to live in any other period of history, largely because of the access most of us have to the best health care humanity has ever experienced.

We tend to take the unspeakable wonders of historic medical break-throughs for granted as we insist desperately on filling the glass all the way up. We lose touch with the sense of awe that Elizabeth Hughes and many others throughout history have had at episodes in what the great physician Sir William Osler called 'man's redemption of man'.

RICHARD BOSWORTH

'It would not be right to have beautiful legends discredited by historical criticism.'

Giovanni Giolitti

This comment was made by Italian Prime Minister Giovanni Giolitti in reply to an unsuccessful request from a historian in June 1912 to publish material from the Piedmontese archives. Giolitti was a liberal, a politician not normally deemed particularly authoritarian. In his old age after 1922 he had a reasonable record in remaining detached from the Fascist dictatorship that took over his country and, in the way of such regimes, strenuously sought to impose a single reading of history onto Italians.

This story has two key aspects. One is its demonstration of the limits of liberalism, a matter to remember today when, ever more completely, we have fallen under the hegemony of some version of neo-liberalism and the 'market'. Now, in my own country, Australia, with its media dominated by Rupert Murdoch, and in the country of my heart, Italy (with ditto by S. Berlusconi), but also in the USA and even in the UK, we are repeatedly told how free we are as individuals to make our own way and take our own opportunities. Yet the gap between rich and poor grows ever wider, despite the obsessive reporting of the momentary fluctuations of equities and currencies and the constant glorification of material gain. In accompaniment, a crass populism is designed to salve any doubts that might occur to those who do not always win.

In this situation, History, too, is often wrenched into service, notably in evoking 'national' military triumphs and tragedies. In his own time, Giolitti was publicly sardonic about the intellectual quality and human understanding of military officers. But in our world of the 'war against terror', we are expected more and more to salute soldiers as our best and brightest. Often this over-patriotic history is merged into heritage and operates outside the academy. But not always.

The second and more important message of the Giolitti story is thus that, now more than ever, History as a discipline needs to remain committed to scanning the past critically. It should unveil what Gibbon might be adapted to call the 'crimes and follies, comedies and tragedies of humankind'. Historians should avoid telling the rich and powerful what they want to hear and, through review of the past, instead help our rulers to stir uneasily at night and contemplate their hypocrisy, rapacity and eventual failure.

ASA BRIGGS

*'We are concerned at the narrowing of the influence of history
in our society, and at its progressive withdrawal from the battle
of ideas. This shrinking of stature cannot be ascribed to a decline
in popular interest . . . "Serious history" has become a subject
reserved for the specialist. The restriction is comparatively
recent. It can be attributed to the consolidation of the historical
profession; to the increasing fragmentation of the subject . . .
and to the narrowness of historians' preoccupations, along with
the way that research is organized and shaped . . . Teaching
and research are increasingly divided, and both divorced from
wider or explicit social purposes . . . We believe that history is
a source of inspiration and understanding, furnishing not only
the means of interpreting the past but also the best critical
vantage point from which to view the present.'*

History Workshop

The study of history has been transformed in my lifetime as an historian;
first a social historian who put the politics in, then a cultural historian. A
pointer to the transformation was the development of History Workshops
at Ruskin College, Oxford. In the spring of 1976 their organisers began to
publish a journal, *History Workshop*, and I still turn back to that first
editorial written by what it called a collective: it still seems to me to be
relevant a generation later.

In itself history teaches us nothing. Yet it is a necessary source of
information that demands explanation and a stimulus both to argument
and to imagination.

KEN BURNS

'The mystic chords of memory, stretching from every battlefield and patriot grave to every living heart and hearthstone all over this broad land, will yet swell the chorus of the Union, when again touched, as surely they will be, by the better angels of our nature.'

Abraham Lincoln, 4 March 1861

K. N. CHAUDHURI

'We spent the night as usual in the open air . . . in a plantation whose owner [Don Ignacio] was hunting jaguars. He was almost naked, and brownish-black like a sambo: *this did not stop him from believing that he was from the caste of whites. He called his wife and daughter, as naked as he was, Dona Isabela and Dona Manuela. Without ever having left the Apure river bank, they took a lively interest "in news from Madrid . . . and that kind of thing from over there* (todas las cosas de alla)*". He knew that the king of Spain would soon come and visit "the great Caracas country", yet he added pleasingly, "As people from the court eat only wheat bread, they would never go beyond the town of Victoria, so we would never see them here." I had brought a chiguire with me . . . but our host assured me that* nostros caballeros blancos *were not born to eat Indian game . . .*

A furious wind rose after midnight . . . we were soaked to the bone . . . Don Ignacio congratulated us on the good fortune of not having slept on the beach but on his land with well bred white people, "entre gente blanca y de trato" . . . What an odd experience it was to find ourselves in these vast solitudes with a man who believed he was European, with all the vain pretensions, hereditary prejudices and mistakes of civilization, but whose only roof was a tree.'

Alexander von Humboldt, *Personal Narrative of a Journey to the Equinoctial Regions of the New Continent*

Humboldt's description and comment is quite entertaining and considering how brief is our journey on earth compared to cosmic time, all human vanities are beside the point, especially the excessively insular psychological disorders of the people of the rain-soaked island that is Britain, skin colour, immigration, broken society, children murdering children, knife culture, alongside Covent Garden Opera, Glyndebourne, Royal Shakespeare Theatre, the list is endless, the inability to utter a word in a language other than the one learned with mother's milk in Coventry and the Gorbals. Everyone dies in the end, some painfully, others in dementia such as Ronald Reagan, some in mortal fear, some in disgrace as Richard Nixon and John Profumo, in torment as Marilyn Monroe, some in beatitude as Augustine of Hippo, and some not knowing what lies on the other side of the Silent River. Antigone in the Theban play of Sophocles was a terrorist for giving her dead brother a decent burial against the orders of the state tyrant. She was walled up alive in a cave and hanged herself. Her betrothed, the son of the state tyrant, committed suicide, not being able to decide his duty between the death of a loving woman and a totally tyrannical state.

For all his liberal views Humboldt could not shake off constantly using expressions like 'among the copper coloured' races. This is exactly the equivalent of the Indian expression used in the sixteenth and seventeenth centuries to describe Europeans as the 'hatmen' or *'gora lok'* ('dusty coloured people'). However, Humboldt was not a racist by any means.

RICHARD COHEN

'History started badly and hav been geting steadily worse. It is like racing really when peason and i have a modest fluter thro the under gardener. All the favourites go down . . . And if you ask all those who hav gone before i am not sure whether they would agree that it is worth it. But it is too late now.

OW TO AVOID HISTORY
No one hav ever found a way of avoiding history it is upon us and around us all. The only thing when you look at the cuning vilaninous faces in ur class you wonder if history may not soon be worse than ever . . . A grate thort strike me:
ALL BOOKS WHICH BOYS HAV TO READ ARE WRONG.'

Geoffrey Willans and Ronald Searle, *The Compleet Molesworth*

Years before Adrian Mole burst upon the scene, here were books that presented what seemed to me then wholly original notions: that history could be funny (it was only later that same year that I was introduced to the Sellar and Yeatman 1930 classic, *1066 And All That*), that historians all had their own agenda, and that what we were taught could be wrong. As Sellar and Yeatman put it, in an axiom that would have had Molesworth's approval if not his spelling, 'History is not what you thought. It is what you can remember.'

On my twelfth birthday I was given a copy of Geoffrey Willans and Ronald Searle's *The Compleet Molesworth*, a compendium of the four best-selling books that they had produced about the rebellious schoolboy Nigel Molesworth and his adventures at St Custard's, an imagined prep school of the early 1950s. Searle would go on to draw the schoolgirls of St Trinians, and Willans was a retired schoolmaster, and between them they had an uncanny knack of capturing the fantasies and fears of schoolchildren then and now. Inevitably, Molesworth considers the teaching and nature of history and makes the above comments.

JOHN ROBERT COLOMBO

'There can hardly be conceived a nationality more destitute of all that can invigorate and elevate a poem, than that which is exhibited by the descendants of the French in Lower Canada, owing to their retaining their peculiar language and manners. They are a people with no history, and no literature.'

Lord Durham, *Report on the Affairs of British North America*

If I had to identify the most potent and prophetic words that have influenced the development of the Dominion of Canada it would be the words that comprise this short passage from Lord Durham's *Report on the Affairs of British North America* (1839). They were written by John Lambton, the English lord known in his day as 'Radical Jack'. Why this outspoken English gentleman along with his entourage was dispatched from London to travel throughout Quebec to study the grievances of the French and the British in the colony in North America has yet to be determined. But he turned out to be the right man at the right time. It is the last ten words from this short passage that drove a stake through the beating heart of Quebec's *ancien régime*, a grievous wound yet in the circumstances not a mortal one. Everyone knows that the vampire always rises from the dead.

The truth of the words – 'no history, and no literature' – so exasperated the Quebec City lawyer François-Xavier Garneau that he devoted considerable time and effort over the next half-dozen years to proving Lord Durham to be wrong – or at least too hasty in his judgement. Those words resulted in the appearance of Garneau's influential *Histoire du Canada* (1845–8), which provided evidence for the rich history and literature of Quebec. Garneau vowed: 'I shall write the history which you do not even know exists. You will see that our ancestors yielded only when outnumbered. There are defeats which are as glorious as victories.' Garneau's rallying cry invigorated the francophone side of the 'two solitudes' and brought it new confidence and respect.

I can think of no more prophetic words of national import, even including Charles de Gaulle's calculated provocation, 'Vive le Québec libre!' uttered from the balcony of Montreal's city hall on 24 July 1967.

PETER CORRIS

*'With history one can never be certain, but I think
I can safely say that Aristotle Onassis would not
have married Mrs Khrushchev.'*

Gore Vidal

This witty remark works as the best humour does – by providing the unexpected. Instead of a weighty, pondered response to a question about global politics, Vidal supplied an apparently flippant, gossipy rejoinder when asked what might have happened had Khrushchev and not Kennedy been assassinated. But his statement has implicit in it serious elements of which Vidal, the brilliant, sceptical social and political commentator, would have been well aware – the empty vanity of a wealthy man requiring a trophy wife, the craving for continual celebrity of an essentially shallow woman and a comment on the enclosed, self-congratulatory world of the rich and powerful.

SAUL DAVID

*'Princes should have more to fear from historians
than have ugly women from great painters.'*

Antonio Pérez

The above quote, written by the Spanish statesman Antonio Pérez in the late sixteenth century, is as pertinent now as it was then, though for princes we should think politicians. Pérez knew what he was talking about. The son of Prince (later King) Philip's secretary, Antonio followed his father into the royal service by becoming Secretary of State of Castile in 1566. But he later fell foul of his royal master, Philip II, when he arranged the murder of the secretary of the King's half-brother, Don Juan of Austria. The secretary had been appointed to spy on Don Juan, whom the King distrusted, and Pérez had him killed when he failed to implicate his employer. But he justified the killing to Philip II by insisting that the secretary was part of a plot to replace him with Don Juan, and when the King discovered the truth he ordered Pérez's arrest. Pérez later escaped and fled to France where he gained his revenge by writing his *Relaciones*, the document which is chiefly responsible for blackening Philip II's memory.

Pérez, of course, had an axe to grind. Most historians do not (or should not). But his point is a good one: a powerful man can try as hard as he likes to burnish his reputation when he is alive, but historians will have the final say. Hitler, Stalin and Mao, three giants of the twentieth century, were revered as great leaders during their lifetimes; and yet all have been exposed by historians as the murderous fanatics they really were. Even rulers more deserving of history's approval, like Lloyd George and JFK, have been shown to have feet of clay. And, though it may be small consolation to the families of the many innocents killed in the recent and ongoing wars in Iraq and Afghanistan, we can be sure that historians will not be kind to the latest world leaders who tried to push their weight around: George W. Bush and Tony Blair.

WILLIAM C. DAVIS

'*You cannot understand your own history when it is the only history you know.*'

Thomas Sowell

Today, when the West finds itself locked in a seemingly hopeless combat with the forces of militant Islam, it is all too easy to succumb to the temptation to yield to stereotype born of ignorance by demonizing whole ethnic and religious groups. The horrors of 11 September 2001 and what has come since are current events already turning into and influencing our history, and yet millions – including our leaders – are most often content to see it in isolation from the history of other peoples. It takes nothing away from the absolutely inexcusable horror of what Al Qaeda has done, to take a serious look at the past few centuries, and especially the first two-thirds of the twentieth century, to look at the forces that led to the creation of this level of militant hatred and resentment, and to try to come to terms with our own unwitting involvement.

Virtually no one in the West now remembers or could explain the mandates that came out of the First World War, or recount with even limited accuracy the story of forces in play that led to the creation of Israel or the expulsion of the Palestinians. Yet these are the defining elements in the creation of militant Islam. Now that the djinn is out of the bottle, understanding what created it will not make it go away, but without that understanding, our natural and often visceral reactions threaten a virtual guarantee that what we do in ignorance of the history of others will only make our history to come more perilous.

TERRY DEARY

'If you think acting is full of queens, you should see the
number of queens among academic archaeologists.
They thought their discipline was being traduced by a
clown. I have more honorary degrees than O-levels and
I always felt I was outside that milieu. But, my God,
it's my right to get inside that stuff.'

Tony Robinson

Spot on, Mr Robinson. Maybe 'queens' is a little too polite an adjective for some of the historians I've encountered. I don't want to argue with another populist 'presenter of history' – I won't demean Mr Robinson by tarring him with the title 'historian' – but maybe 'pompous, self-righteous, self-serving, arrogant, devious, immature, patronizing queens', would be more accurate?

CARLO D'ESTE

'Let us learn our lessons. Never, never, never believe any war will be smooth or easy, or that anyone who embarks on the strange voyage can measure the tides and hurricanes he will encounter. The Statesman who yields to war fever must realize that once the signal is given, he is no longer master of policy but the slave of unforeseeable and uncontrollable events.'

Winston Churchill, *My Early Life*

Churchill's prescient warning of the out-of-control consequences for those who instigate war is timeless. Here are two modern-day examples, one positive, the other negative. General Dwight D. Eisenhower made one of the most important decisions of the Second World War: the order to carry out the D-Day landings on 6 June 1944 in uncertain weather conditions. Having done so, Eisenhower was incapable of either reversing it or altering in any way the outcome of the invasion, which was now in other hands. His immediate role was irrelevant.

While Eisenhower fully understood the consequences of his decision, President George W. Bush did not when he ordered the invasion of Iraq in 2003 on the basis of flawed intelligence and even more flawed motives. Bush seems to have had no concept of what he had unleashed, for which history will ultimately pass a harsh sentence. Unfortunately, Churchill's words have repeatedly gone unheeded by politicians who pose as statesmen but lack foresight.

TAYLOR DOWNING

'We shall all be judged by history . . . and I shall write the history.'

Winston Churchill

On several occasions Churchill advised friends and colleagues to wait for the verdict of history, adding with a smile that he would write that history. And indeed he did write a lot of history. Millions of words poured out, ranging from his earliest histories of the campaigns he witnessed, in Malakand and the Sudan, to the biography of his father; from the massive five-volume history of the First World War, *The World Crisis*, to his six-volume history, *The Second World War*; from portraits of friends and heroes in *Great Contemporaries* to the huge biography of his ancestor Marlborough, to his even more vast *History of the English-Speaking Peoples*.

In the histories of events in which he had participated, which are of most interest today, Churchill always placed himself at the centre of the story. Bonar Law described *The World Crisis* cruelly but amusingly as 'an auto-biography disguised as a history of the universe'! He didn't work like a professional historian and would always start with a clear idea of what he wanted to say. 'Give me the facts,' he told Maurice Ashley, one of his assistants on the Marlborough epic, 'and I will twist them the way I want to suit my argument.' His books were always immensely readable. Like free-flowing rivers they poured forth, bubbling with great stories and vivid characters, all borne along by the driving current of narrative. But Churchill's view of history was like a religious faith to him and at the core of his outlook on the world. The institutions of British government had emerged over time around a belief in liberty and freedom. And he believed Britain had a special destiny in coming to the aid of Europe when it was threatened by the shadow of tyranny. Such beliefs sustained him and helped him sustain the British people through the dark days of 1940 and 1941.

Churchill's Whiggish view of history is totally unfashionable today and his histories are rarely consulted other than to give an insight into his own partisan view on events. But they do show how an interpretation of history can help when the chips are down. And they are a great reminder of the power of narrative history. Sometimes, history really is too important to be left to historians.

JONATHAN EIG

'You can get a lot farther with a smile and a gun than you can get with just a smile.'

Alphonse Capone

This quote reminds me of the famous Teddy Roosevelt line, 'Speak softly and carry a big stick.' But I think Capone said it better. Capone's gangster career was surprisingly brief, running for a mere decade, and his time at the top of the Chicago outfit was even briefer, spanning five years, from 1926 to 1931. He was only twenty-seven years old when he acquired power and fame and thirty-two when he went to prison on charges of income-tax evasion.

Most people assume that Capone needed only the gun to make his mark, but, in fact, I would argue that his smile – and he had a genuinely winning one – played an important role, too. For all his violent tendencies, Capone was a gregarious man. People liked working and carousing with him, so long as they stayed on his good side. And the press utterly adored him. He gave in-depth interviews in which he defended his career path, begged for the public's empathy, and fired off shots at the hypocritical politicians who passed and routinely flouted the Prohibition laws that made criminals rich.

Only in America's Roaring Twenties, when the nation went wild and celebrities led the way, could a man like Capone admit he was a violent criminal and yet bask so luxuriantly in the spotlight's warm glow.

He had guts. He had style. And, yes, he had a gun. With those things, he conquered a city and captivated a nation.

JOHN ELLIOTT

'I have loved the Mediterranean with passion, no doubt because I am a northerner like so many others in whose footsteps I have followed.'

Fernand Braudel, *The Mediterranean and the Mediterranean World*

The opening words of Fernand Braudel's great work *The Mediterranean and the Mediterranean World in the Age of Philip II* are the public confession of a private passion – a passion, as he says, felt by many another northerner, before and after him. I count myself among those who have felt that passion, but as a historian I found that it was reinforced by my reading of Braudel's book, which opened my eyes to wonderful possibilities. What Braudel tried to do was to write a 'total history' of the Mediterranean world in the sixteenth century, drawing on a vast range of sources that would throw light on its geographical features, and on the economic and social forces that shaped the societies which bordered the sea. All this material, full of remarkable insights and fascinating nuggets of information, occupied the first two sections of his massive book, and was intended to provide a context for understanding the succession of events that would culminate in the encounter of the Spanish and Ottoman empires – of Christendom versus Islam – at the Battle of Lepanto on the waters of the Mediterranean in 1571.

Braudel's enterprise was vastly ambitious, and has proved enormously influential. It encouraged me, like other historians of my generation, to aspire to the writing of 'total history', in place of the dominant political narrative of much contemporary historical writing, and of the tendency to keep social and economic history in distinct compartments. But how successful was Braudel in realizing this noble ambition? The book has its flaws, and these have become more apparent with the passage of time. Heavily influenced by the pervasive Marxism of the immediate post-war years, Braudel's depiction leaves little space for the impact of human agency in the face of impersonal economic forces. Nor does it leave much space for the cultural differences between the Muslim and Christian societies that ringed the sea. His Mediterranean has an artificial unity, and at times it becomes an almost mystical entity with independent powers of action, as when he writes: 'The truth is that the Mediterranean has struggled against a fundamental poverty'. But to a historian who loved the Mediterranean with such passion, much can be forgiven.

RICHARD VAN EMDEN

*'To my son Coco, his friends, and their mothers, I offer
this simple record of the dark caravan that winds
endlessly through the memory of my youth.'*

**Shirley Millard, *I Saw Them Die: Diary and
Recollections of Shirley Millard***

No quotation or phrase encapsulates so adroitly, and in so few words, the colossal volume of emotional baggage bequeathed by the Great War. They are the closing lines of the war memoirs of an American nurse, sending us all not only a poignant reminder that those who die are no more the victims of war than those who are left behind, but also that eventual peace, even peace with victory, still leaves an unfathomable, dark legacy of misery for countless souls for whom life is, and will remain forever, tainted.

Nurse Millard's words are pregnant with dignity and emotion. She lost no one blood-related, or so it seems, but she did not have to in order to give authority to her thoughts. She was a parent by proxy to the lads whose hands she held in their last moments, as much a mother then as the blood mothers to whom she wrote letters of condolence hours later.

To a post-war world, there was perhaps some solace in knowing that such loss was common to the community, replicated many times over in neighbouring streets. Memorials to the dead were erected and the two-minute silence observed by all. For many, it was not only a matter of remembering the dead but also a chance to reflect on the sacrifices of those who had survived. The survivors: haunted by the missing, bodies never found or identified; survivors driven to despair by the thought of a loved one's lingering death; survivors forced to carry on despite the loss of every child, and the consigning to the grave of a family's aspirations and dreams.

It is only right that the dead are remembered and venerated, but the living were all too frequently abandoned to struggle on in poverty and isolation. The only really tangible reminders today of the pain of the Great War are the epitaphs carved on the soldiers' graves that give some clue to the enormity of the loss. These words, privately paid for by families – at no cost to a grateful nation – are now all that remind us that, of course, countless thousands of dark caravans wound their way through the country lanes and narrow streets of Britain's post-war collective memory, all making their own lonely and meandering way to nowhere, for there was no escape from loss and no escape from recall; no such thing as closure for anyone.

JOHN ENGLISH

'I cannot rewrite history. It is our purpose to be just in our time and that is what we have done in bringing in the Charter of Rights.'

Pierre Trudeau

When Pierre Trudeau became prime minister of Canada in 1968, he seemingly represented a sharp break with the country's conservative past. Mark Kurlansky's history of the upheavals of 1968, 'the birth of our postmodern media-driven world', portrays Trudeau as emblematic of a new approach to leadership 'where a figure is known by style rather than substance'.

Two generations later the impact of Trudeau on Canada is controversial, although both foes and friends argue that it was substantial. His constitutional reforms, which included a charter of rights, fundamentally altered the role of Canadian courts. His critics, especially in English Canada, charge that he swept away their Anglo-Canadian traditions with an American approach to law, identity and history.

Trudeau deliberately created an air of mystery surrounding his own past, and it is unsurprising that contemporary analyses now seem to have widely missed the mark. When he took office in 1968, he presented himself as a foe of 'nationalism', an outdated and dangerous emotion whose Quebec advocates he denounced as reactionaries. Yet we now know that Trudeau himself was a Quebec separatist willing to accept violence to advance the cause during the early years of World War II and that his own nationalism lingered into the 1950s. Moreover, Trudeau brazenly used pan-Canadian nationalism in his final election campaign in the winter of 1979–80.

There was, nonetheless, one area where he remained consistent throughout his political career: Trudeau adamantly refused to permit the state to provide redress for historical wrongs. Most famously, he would neither apologize to Japanese Canadians for their internment in the Second World War nor offer redress to Chinese Canadians for mistreatment in earlier times. With aboriginal Canadians, Trudeau's first response was a White Paper that promised to end the reserves and make them citizens like other Canadians, an offer they firmly rebuffed. We can, he declared, only be 'just in our time'.

Trudeau's Conservative successor Brian Mulroney characteristically rejected Trudeau's approach and gave an apology and compensation to

Japanese Canadians. Not surprisingly, similar approaches soon followed with Chinese Canadians, Ukrainian Canadians, and, in a more complex fashion, aboriginal Canadians. Trudeau did not endorse these policies.

Many observers trace Trudeau's opposition to redress of grievances to his obdurate focus on individual rather than group rights, a stance he expressed constantly in the argument for a charter of rights. There is merit in the arguments, but Trudeau himself did not express them clearly. His own opposition was expressed in his sense of history and, one suspects, his personal experiences.

Trudeau came of political age when the British conquest of Quebec was a lively historical issue, one that fuelled Quebec nationalism and separatism at mid-century. Rather than a 'happy calamity', the description of Harvard historian Frances Parkman of how the French defeat brought British liberty to Quebec, many Quebec historians spoke of the 'decapitation' of a vibrant New France and the yoke of British oppression. Earlier traditional historians had celebrated the role of the Catholic Church in maintaining the French culture and faith.

For Trudeau in the fifties this celebration of a distant and, in his view, false past served the autocratic Duplessis government of Quebec with its ties to a conservative and still repressive Church. 'Open up the windows', Trudeau declaimed, the people of Quebec were suffocating. Trudeau presented himself as a liberalizing force in those times, and nationalism, with its close association with Quebec's history, imprisoned Quebec in its own past. He called for a 'functionalism' which would bring modern social science to the challenges Quebec faced.

His wariness of the burdens of the past and his tendency to link other issues to the Quebec experience made Trudeau suspicious of other attempts to obtain redress. Where would it stop? By casting away the past, Canadians could forge a truth appropriate for their own times. A supporter of Vatican II in the early sixties and a fervent opponent of Quebec nationalists whose arguments were laced with strong doses of resentment against past wrongs, Trudeau argued that we could only be 'just in our time'. Only then could we escape history's heavy hand.

CHARLES ESDAILE

*'History is the version of past events that people
have decided to agree upon.'*

Napoleon Bonaparte

As a specialist in the Napoleonic period, I suppose that I was always likely to turn to Napoleon when asked to come up with a quote about history. The fact that I have chosen the one I cite here, however, does not mean that I agree with it. On the contrary, it is an idea that, like most things that Napoleon stood for, I abhor, for, were it true, then the pursuit of the past would be utterly pointless. Still worse, the emperor would finally have won his war, and that is something that I will never accept or, perhaps more accurately, cease to contest.

Quoted in the abstract, perhaps, the comment does not appear so challenging: after all, cultural historians have long argued that what matters is not so much what happened in the past, but rather how the past is perceived, recorded and interpreted. Yet this has always seemed to me a counsel of despair: we may never ever be able to establish for certain the exact chronology of a particular event or the reasons why certain things happened, but professional historians should surely never cease to challenge established nostra, to strive for a more exact understanding of the past and to seek to inform a wider public of their findings. Apart from anything else, to do otherwise runs the risk of allowing evil of all sorts to flourish, for few things have had greater power to wreak havoc amongst mankind than historical myths.

However, in this particular instance, of course, Napoleon was not speaking in the abstract. On the contrary, what he was really saying was not so much that history was the version of past events that people decided to agree upon, but rather that history was the version of past events, and, specifically, of his own times, that he had decided they should believe. Perhaps more keenly aware of the need to legitimise his rule in the eyes of posterity than almost any other statesman of the modern era, from the very earliest days of his rule he sought to create a positive image of himself and to ensure that it was that image by which he was remembered.

In this, moreover, he was extraordinarily successful: when my students come to my third-year option on the French Revolution and Napoleon they invariably do so with ingrained notions of the emperor as a champion of freedom and democracy who was brought down by the inveterate hostility of a vengeful *ancien régime*. In this I am sure that they are not alone – if Napoleon did not enjoy a generally positive image, he would not be employed with quite such regularity by the advertising industry. But, to take another quote from Napoleon, the emperor also called history 'a set of lies agreed upon'. In the case of the Napoleonic legend, nothing could be closer to the truth, and thus it is that I feel doubly certain that the quote must be raised only in order to bring it, most literally perhaps, to book. Yet, say this though I do, Napoleon's latter-day *Grande Armée* of admirers can at least take comfort in the fact that my guns are trained, not just on the legend of Saint Helena, but on all legends without distinction: as a hispanist, for example, I have fought particularly hard to combat the idea that the whole of Spain rose body and soul against Napoleon in 1808, and have been able to suggest pretty unequivocally that the reality was very different. If history is the version of past events that people have decided to agree upon, then historians are those men and women brave or foolhardy enough to challenge those same ideas and 'by opposing end them'.

RICHARD J. EVANS

'And with regard to my factual reporting of the events of the war I have made it a principle not to write down the first story that came my way, and not even to be guided by my own general impressions; either I was present myself at the events which I have described or else I heard of them from eyewitnesses whose reports I have checked with as much thoroughness as possible. Not that even so the truth was easy to discover. Different eyewitnesses give different accounts of the same events, speaking out of partiality for one side or the other or else from imperfect memories. And it may well be that my history will seem less easy to read because of the absence in it of a romantic element. It will be enough for me, however, if these words of mine are judged useful by those who want to understand clearly the events which happened in the past and which (human nature being what it is) will at some time or other and in much the same ways, be repeated in the future. My work is not a piece of writing designed to meet the taste of an immediate public, but was done to last for ever.'

Thucydides

My favourite quote comes from the introductory section of Thucydides' *The Peloponnesian War*, written in the fifth century BCE, where he lays out his method and approach to writing the history of the ruinous war between Athens and Sparta that began in 431 BCE and in which he was himself a participant.

This seems to me to capture admirably both the ambition of the true historian and the difficulties faced in achieving it. Of course, Thucydides does not pursue his purpose in modern style; he has no footnotes, he does not identify his sources, and he seldom informs us whether he was or was not present at the events he describes. He relies on eyewitness accounts and not on original documents, which came to be prized above all other sources by professional historians from the nineteenth century onwards. Nevertheless, he rigorously excludes the 'romantic' myths so beloved of his predecessor Herodotus, and he is acutely aware of the fallibility of memory and the unreliability of his sources. He is clear that the historian's purpose is above all to explain and understand the past.

And as for his final, breathtakingly ambitious claim, it is one all historians secretly harbour, I suspect, but one which we know at the same time is unrealizable, because our work is all to soon superseded by new discoveries and new interpretations.

AMANDA FOREMAN

'Don't read History to me, for I know that can't be true.'
Sir Robert Walpole

Sir Robert Walpole was Great Britain's first prime minister and remains to this day its longest serving. During his twenty-one years in power he steadfastly kept to his policy of peace abroad and low taxes at home. But his methods earned him many enemies and there were few lamentations when he retired in 1742 with an earldom and one of the great art collections of Europe. (Both were gone within three generations.) Walpole's comment on History was in answer to his son's question as to which book he should read aloud. It speaks to the heart of the historian's dilemma. Walpole was not claiming that History was all lies – he was simply stating that so much of what really influences politics takes place behind the scenes. He knew that official explanations of momentous decisions or moments often disguised a far more serpentine reality. Petty dramas and low emotions such as vanity, revenge or greed often played as great a part in the formation of ministries as any of the formal levers of politics. A generation later, Georgiana, Duchess of Devonshire, commented that 'the secret springs of events are seldom known. But when they are, they become particularly instructive and entertaining.' This, then, is the challenge to the historian: to uncover these 'secret springs' so that the facts and the truth are one and the same.

MARTIN GILBERT

'No more war.'

Winston Churchill

By 1930, Winston Churchill had been an active politician for thirty years. On the outbreak of the First World War, he was First Lord of the Admiralty. When the war ended, he was Minister of Munitions. After his temporary political demise in May 1915 following the failure of the naval attack on the Dardanelles, he had begun writing his own account of the First World War, later published in five volumes as *The World Crisis*, with a sixth volume entitled *The Aftermath*.

When, in 1930, his friend Lord Beaverbrook sent him his own book, *Politicians and the War*, describing the outbreak and early course of the war, Churchill wrote to him: 'What a tale. Think of all these people, decent, educated. Patriotic, loyal, clean, decent, trying their utmost: what a ghastly muddle they made of it. Unteachable from infancy to tomb, this is the first and last characteristic of mankind.'

Having signed this letter, Churchill wrote at the bottom: 'No more war'. But, as he himself had written, mankind was unteachable.

HERMANN GILIOMEE

*'History is a story, a story needs a narrator and a
narrator needs to be standing somewhere.
The view from nowhere does not work.'*

Tony Judt

In 1992, as the Afrikaner ruling group in South Africa was preparing to
transfer power to the African National Congress, I embarked on a history
of the Afrikaners.

What kind of history would people want to read in hoping to learn about
the Afrikaner past and in particular their dominant role in the imposition

of apartheid, a universally abhorred system? My assumption was that people want a story told in a particular way. Tony Judt, one of the most interesting contemporary historians, made the above remark.

I decided that I would write not as an Afrikaner historian but as an historian who is an Afrikaner, in the spirit of Graham Greene, who said he was not a Catholic writer but a writer who is a Catholic. I saw my challenge as that of writing with empathy and understanding without condoning or explaining away the injustices the Afrikaners perpetrated. In the book's introduction, written late in 2002, I cited the words of F. D. H. Kitto, a historian of Greece in antiquity: 'To understand is not necessarily to pardon, but there is no harm in trying to understand.'

This statement is not quite the safe position it seems, as was pointed out by Neville Alexander, a literary scholar and political activist who spent ten years on Robben Island along with prisoners like Nelson Mandela. Speaking at the launch of my book *The Afrikaners: Biography of a People* in 2003, he responded to Kitto's words by citing Madame De Staël's '*tout comprendre rend très indulgent*'. *The Concise Oxford Dictionary of Quotations* translates this as: 'To be totally understanding makes one very indulgent.' One could also say 'too indulgent'. Alexander's comment highlights the very fine but also very important line between apology and empathy.

DONALD E. GRAVES

'Of all national assets archives are the most precious; they are the gift of one generation to another and the extent of our care of them marks the extent of our civilization.'

Sir Arthur G. Doughty

These words are inscribed on the memorial statue of Arthur Doughty, which is located behind the Library and Archives building in Ottawa, overlooking the broad Ottawa River. They summarize Doughty's lifetime efforts as an historian and archivist to collect, organize and preserve the records of the past for the future.

Born at Maidenhead, Arthur Doughty was educated at public schools and Oxford before emigrating to Montreal in 1886 where he entered the commercial world. He was a very keen amateur poet and prominent in the city's literary circles and as a drama critic. In 1897 he joined the civil service of the Province of Quebec and became the legislative librarian in 1901.

When a controversy arose over the exact location of the 1759 Battle of the Plains of Abraham, Doughty began to research the subject and, with G. W. Parmelee, edited a six-volume collection, *The Siege of Quebec and the Battle of the Plains of Abraham*, in 1901. His work on this subject drew Doughty's attention to the neglected state of Canada's national archives and he was appointed Dominion Archivist.

Until his retirement in 1935 Doughty worked tirelessly at creating the Public Archives of Canada and turning it into a dynamic and professional institution. He directed the organization of records and manuscripts, sought out significant private collections and manuscripts, rare posters and art, and directed the transcription of records in London and Paris.

One of the more unusual tasks he undertook came during the First World War when he became involved in the distribution of war trophies. Thousands of German artillery pieces, mortars, machine guns and small arms were shipped to Canada, catalogued and then distributed across the country to places where many of them can still be seen today. Among the trophies was a sizeable collection of war art and a number of operational aircraft.

Doughty promoted the creation of provincial archives across Canada and edited several document collections, including the monumental 23-volume *Canada and its Provinces*. Doughty died in 1936 and was honoured with a statue, one of only two in Ottawa dedicated to civil servants. Sir Arthur Doughty's words above ring completely true and the need to preserve the records – paper, film or electronic, and monuments it might be added – of one generation for future generations is even more pressing in light of the rapid development that has occurred since the 1930s.

CHARLOTTE GRAY

'The past is never dead. In fact, it's not even past.'

William Faulkner

The characters in William Faulkner's novels often don't realize how much they are products of family and context, living out scripts written by their forebears. Countries can also be unaware of the power of past scripts. When I moved from England to Canada in 1980, I was bewildered to find myself in a country with no unified national narrative, no revolutionary creation story and few historical shrines.

Perhaps, I reflected, the past can have little to do with the present when the population is in a constant churn. Canada has been peopled by the First Nations, who have lived on its harsh landscape for centuries, and successive waves of immigration. British and French settlers arrived before Confederation in 1867, followed in the late nineteenth and early twentieth centuries by eastern and southern Europeans. After the Second World War came a surge from the Caribbean, and most recently crowds of Chinese, Koreans and North Africans. Some of the settlers arrived as immigrants, eager to make a new start in the New World. Others came as refugees, desperate to escape cruel regimes.

Newcomers bring their own stories. Historical studies here are a subsidiary of 'Social Studies' in schools, and a footnote in 'Citizenship Education' for new Canadians. Hockey, not history, appears to be the national glue. At a conscious level, most Canadians have a shaky grasp of such key historical facts as the name of the first prime minister (Sir John A. Macdonald) or the date when Canada brought home its constitution from Westminster (1982).

But then I realized that the lived experience of being Canadian has been shaped by all those layers of immigration. The Canadian past is embedded in the collective unconscious here. The deep tradition of 'reasonable accommodation', first between English- and French-speaking Canadians, and then between established Canadians and newcomers, has spawned attitudes of tolerance that characterize this country.

Canada's uniqueness lies in its identity as a bilingual, multicultural country that participates in every international peacekeeping operation. There have been internal traumas, but conflict is resolved, new traditions (Mounties in turbans, same-sex marriage) are accepted, and the country moves on . . . Faulkner's characters were trapped by history; Canadians are part of a dynamic present. But in both cases, the past is far from dead.

TOM GRIFFITHS

'The most unhistorical thing we can do is to imagine that the past is us in funny clothes.'

Greg Dening

Greg Dening was a remarkable historian and anthropologist of the Pacific and with these words he is reminding us that writing history always involves a voyage across cultures. Our double historical quest is to be astonished as well as to understand. This tension goes to the heart of the historical enterprise – a tension between the past as familiar (and continuous with our own experience) and the past as strange (and therefore able to widen our understanding of what it means to be human). The essence of good history is this balance between empathy and perspective, between intimacy and distance. Historians move constantly between reading and thinking their way into the lives and minds of the people of the past – giving them back their present with all its future possibilities – and seeing them from afar, with a bracing sense of their strangeness. The discipline of history is required to help us discover what we cannot instinctively feel or see.

CHRIS HALE

'Hegel remarks somewhere that all great world-historic facts and personages appear, so to speak, twice. He forgot to add: the first time as tragedy, the second time as farce . . . Men make their own history, but they do not make it as they please; they do not make it under self-selected circumstances, but under circumstances existing already, given and transmitted from the past. The tradition of all dead generations weighs like a nightmare on the brains of the living . . . Thus Luther put on the mask of the Apostle Paul, the Revolution of 1789–1814 draped itself alternately in the guise of the Roman Republic and the Roman Empire . . . Cromwell and the English people had borrowed from the Old Testament the speech, emotions, and illusions for their bourgeois revolution. When the real goal had been achieved and the bourgeois transformation of English society had been accomplished, Locke supplanted Habakkuk.'

Karl Marx, *The 18th Brumaire of Louis Napoleon*

We have lost sight of Karl Marx's brilliance as an historian. Since the collapse of Communism after 1989, Marx's reputation has been clouded by a blame game that attributes the crimes of Stalin and Mao to a nineteenth-century German political philosopher. This is both unjust and unintelligent. There is beauty in the idea that the unfolding of history begins as tragedy but ends as farce. We would surely agree that 'men make their own history, but they do not make it as they please'. In that one pungent phrase, Marx pins down the human tragedy. 'The tradition of all dead generations weighs like a nightmare on the brains of the living.' The poetic arc of this thrilling sentence compels admiration, anticipating perhaps the dilemma of modern socialists.

Any one of the ideas that spark from the pages of Marx's little pamphlet could provide inspiration for an essay or a book: 'Cromwell and the English people had borrowed from the Old Testament the speech, emotions, and illusions for their bourgeois revolution. When the real goal had been achieved and the bourgeois transformation of English society had been accomplished, Locke supplanted Habakkuk.' This pithy synopsis of a turning point in our history sets out a veritable feast of ideas – and imaginative ideas are sorely needed in modern history writing.

PHILIP HAYTHORNTHWAITE

'When civilians write military history, and venture to advance opinions of their own on technical points of which the Profession alone are able to judge, they, generally, talk nonsense; as Mr Alison does on such subjects in the course of his (otherwise) interesting work.'

Anon. ('A General Officer')

The Napoleonic Wars provided a catalyst for the growth in the production of works of specifically military history, and a military readership, notably an officer corps, of increasing professionalism. The veracity of some of the contemporary works was not unquestioned by those who regarded military history as the preserve of military experts, which led to the comment above on the work of Sir Archibald Alison. Writing in *Colburn's United Service Magazine and Military Journal*, the critic signed himself 'A General Officer' and commented on Alison's egregious ignorance.

Conversely, comments by 'the Profession' could be equally misleading – as the Duke of Wellington complained about letters written home by officers during the Peninsular War, everyone who could write and who had a friend who could read would write an account of what he did not know and comment about what he did not understand. With such strictures in mind, it is interesting to observe the reaction to a military expert who did attempt to produce a researched history. William Siborne's *History of the War in France and Belgium in 1815* was one of the most significant early studies of the Waterloo campaign but a review in *Colburn's United Service Magazine* found it too much of a history; the reviewer commented on 'that vast procession of names . . . which in Captain Siborne's pages march before us . . . But, unfortunately, very few readers have a memory capable of retaining so many names; nor can their wish be very great to remember numerous names of men they never heard of before – names, too (many of them), of excessive length, and so rugged as to defy pronunciation by English lips. Capt. Siborne, different from us, seems to be fond of these long unspeakable names, all of which he takes care to give at full length; not a Von is omitted . . . our heads turn dizzy with endeavouring to remember them . . . We hope that Capt. Siborne is preparing an abridgement of his work, which we are sure will be more useful than the massive original. In that case, nine out of ten of these hard names will, no doubt, be omitted.'

JOHN HEMMING

'I now see that you French are great madmen . . . Is the land that nourished you not sufficient? We have fathers, mothers and children whom we love. But we are certain that after our death the land that nourished us will also feed them. We therefore rest without further cares.'

Jean de Lery

My main historical writing has been about the conquest of South America by Europeans – the Incas overthrown by Pizarro's conquistadors; civilizations of northern South America invaded by desperadoes searching for the gold of El Dorado; and the absorption of hundreds of indigenous peoples in what is now Brazil. In all of these, only the European side had writing, so all historical records and chronicles are from the conquerors' perspective. And there are contrasting mind-sets: Europeans obsessed with facts, figures, names and dates; American Indians with Homeric traditions in which memory and mythology blend to form cultural heritage.

Native Americans are eloquent orators, but their speeches were recorded all too rarely and then, of course, only in the foreign language of the intruders. The French Protestant pastor Jean de Lery recorded in the 1550s a wise indigenous chief comparing the two races' attitudes to property. He marvelled that the French made arduous voyages to Brazil just to obtain brazilwood dye-wood; he wondered why a French trader would want to accumulate quantities of this and, when he died, leave it to his children.

Over four centuries later, in 1988, the Kayapo woman Tuira challenged an electrical engineer who wanted to inundate much of her people's land with a hydroelectric dam. 'We don't need electricity. Electricity will not give us food. We need the rivers to flow freely – our future depends on them. We need our forests to hunt and gather in.' When the engineer argued that the dam would bring prosperity, she answered: 'Don't talk to us about relieving our "poverty". We are not poor: we are the richest people in Brazil. We are not wretched. We are Indians.'

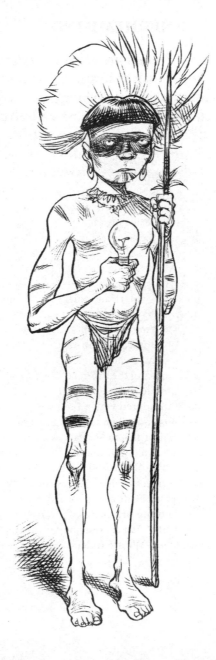

ERIC HOBSBAWM

'Men make their own history, but they do not make it just as they please; they do not make it under circumstances chosen by themselves, but under circumstances directly encountered, given and transmitted from the past. The tradition of all the dead generations weighs like a nightmare on the brain of the living.'

Karl Marx, *The 18th Brumaire of Louis Napoleon*

I have chosen this quotation because it is particularly relevant today when practically all groups of people and new states construct themselves a self-serving mythology based on their supposed identity with a misunderstood and sometimes invented past. For this reason sceptical historians have never been more required than in the past forty years.

JAMES HOLLAND

'History will be kind to me, for I intend to write it.'

Winston Churchill

And he certainly did – he was a prolific writer, not least of his six-volume history of the Second World War. I am a great admirer of Churchill for many reasons – after all he did save Britain and arguably the world in 1940 – but his ability to produce memorable one-line quips was just one of his many talents. Beneath the wit, most held nuggets of wisdom, as is the case with this gem. Facts are facts, but history is the study of who created those facts and why. This makes it, in essence, the study of human nature and personality, and individual decision-making. Everything boils down to that, and so any conclusions by a historian are necessarily subjective because only the individual can really ever know what was going on inside his head. Yet history is also the process by which we record the past, which requires a decision as to what to include and what to leave out, which is similarly a subjective decision. And, of course, *The Second World War* Volumes I–VI is kind to Churchill, but like all the best history, it is also hugely entertaining.

RICHARD HOLMES

*'Several of the Staff were standing in the street, when a motor-
car drove up coming from the north. It proceeded slowly round
the place towards the Church steps on which General Lanrezac
was standing. In it reclined a badly wounded man, with a face
the colour of ashes. On seeing General Lanrezac, he made a sign
and the car stopped. Many officers recognized General Boé,
commanding the 20th Division belonging to the X Corps.
The wounded man made another sign. His hand lifted as if to
salute, but dropped and hung over the door . . . The Chief of
Staff stepped quickly forward, almost ran to the car, and clasped
Boé's hand. He did not speak. Boé was silent for a moment,
looking towards Lanrezac. Then he whispered – "Tell him,"
he gasped, then, speaking louder as he realized that Hély
d'Oissel could hardly hear him, he repeated, "Tell the General
we held on as long as we could." His head fell back, his eyes
were very sad. Hély d'Oissel grasped his hand again and said
nothing. Still General Lanrezac had not moved. The car grated
into gear, and drove slowly on.'*

Edward Spears

We cannot really, really understand a battle without seeing the field on
which it was fought; nor can we fully grasp the nature of command without
understanding where generals positioned themselves, how they gleaned
information and how they transmitted their orders. In August 1914
Lieutenant Edward Spears was on a brief attachment to the French War
Ministry. After the outbreak of war he was posted to the most northerly of
the French armies, General Charles Lanrezac's Fifth, as liaison officer
between it and the British Expeditionary Force, which was to come into
line on its left.

On 22 August, arguably the bloodiest day in French history, with red-
trousered infantrymen falling in windrows from Alsace to Belgium, Fifth
Army gave battle on the line of the River Sambre astride Charleroi. It was
bundled off the river-crossings and forced back southwards by a tactically
more adept enemy, despite the sometimes suicidal bravery of its soldiers.

Lanrezac's main headquarters was in the Belgian town of Chimay, and
he had established a forward command post in the smaller town of Mettet,
about 12 kilometres behind the river. There, Spears heard that the French

infantry had been 'taken aback' by the fire of German heavy howitzers, but there appeared to be 'little or no definite news'.

It was not poor Boé's wounds that made such a tragic impression on the minds of all those who saw him at Mettet, though they were bad enough, a bullet through the arm and another through the stomach. It was the despair in his face that moved them. He was thinking of his men, and the sight of his emotion conjured up a vision of the division which had suffered so severely that even its commander had been stricken by rifle fire. On the following day Lanrezac recognized that the battle was lost and ordered a general retreat, which the British were to remember as the Retreat from Mons. Lanrezac was dismissed on 3 September: Spears ended the war a brigadier-general and a knight.

HAROLD HOLZER

'We cannot escape history.'
Abraham Lincoln

With this bold declaration to a war-weary United States Congress on 1 December 1862, President Abraham Lincoln called on the legislative branch of his endangered government to do nothing less than change the rationale for fighting secession and rebellion – by widening the net of human freedom. To do less, he declared in this extraordinary warning, would condemn them in the history books for eternity.

Some background: For more than a year, Lincoln had fought a Civil War, he insisted, merely to reunite the American Union as it was. Three months earlier, however, he had issued an Emancipation Proclamation declaring all slaves in Rebel territory free as of 1 January 1863. Now he wanted Congress to do even more: compensate slave-owners to hasten emancipation in the still-loyal Border States, and fund voluntary colonization for freed blacks. Lincoln forwarded these proposals in his annual message to Congress – the equivalent of today's presidential State of the Union address, but unlike modern media extravaganzas, delivered by messenger, not in person.

The message produced this thunderbolt anyway. The war would be transformed, Lincoln said, and liberty granted. Those who supported his position would be remembered in national memory; those who resisted, presumably, forgotten or damned.

It turned out to be a brilliant tactic for softening legislative resistance. 'We of this Congress and this administration will be remembered in spite of ourselves,' he added to the famous phrase with which he began his conclusion. 'The fiery trial through which we pass, will light us down, in honor or dishonor, to the latest generation.'

Congress did not step up to the challenge right away, failing to pursue Lincoln's proposals. It did nothing on compensating loyal slave-owners, and little on the quickly discredited notion of colonization – fortunately for Lincoln's reputation. Eventually, under pressure from the President, it did even more: a constitutional amendment ending slavery everywhere.

Not surprisingly, Lincoln gets most of history's credit. His 'plain, peaceful, generous, just' course, he predicted, was one that 'the world will forever applaud, and God must forever bless'. To the phrasemakers belong the laurels. Modern leaders should take a lesson from Lincoln's audacious claim – not only to history's judgment, but to serve as history's judge. On the other hand, based on recent presidents' almost promiscuous claims to Lincoln, perhaps they shouldn't.

MICHAEL HOWARD

'All history teaches . . .'

Anon.

When anyone begins a sentence with the words 'All history teaches', I know that we are about to hear bad history and worse logic.

I do not know who first said this, but we should all, laymen as well as historians, have the words graven on our hearts. 'History' is simply what historians write, and historians are as liable to error, misjudgement and prejudice as all the rest of mankind. Out of their combined efforts a consensus may emerge, but it must be constantly revisited and revised by subsequent generations. History is constantly changing. To try to build firm conclusions on it is like trying to build a house on running water.

DANIEL W. HOWE

'When in the course of human events, it becomes necessary for one portion of the family of man to assume among the people of the earth a position different from that which they have hitherto occupied, but one to which the laws of nature and of nature's God entitle them, a decent respect for the opinions of mankind requires that they should declare the causes that impel them to such a course.'

Opening of the Declaration issued by the Women's Rights Convention, Seneca Falls, New York, July 1848

This 'Declaration of Sentiments' by the first convention to address the issue of rights for women went on to endorse equal opportunities for education and employment, equal rights in marriage to property, child custody, and divorce, and the elective franchise. It is deliberately modelled on Thomas Jefferson's Declaration of Independence of the United States of America of 1776, and appeals to the same theory of natural rights as formulated by John Locke in the late seventeenth century. It illustrates the importance of social movements grounding their demands in an intellectual framework that commands widespread assent. It demonstrates how the idea of natural rights in particular can be applied not only to nations but also to social groups within a nation. It anticipates the kinds of arguments that would also be used to justify equal political and civil rights for black Americans, and later still by movements for equal rights by other social groups like gays, the disabled, and the aged. In recent years the concept of natural rights, although very far from enjoying a consensus among philosophers, has come to enjoy a degree of practical acceptance among the general public throughout the Western World and even beyond, such that many parties and causes find its invocation necessary.

JOHN HUGHES-WILSON

'In times of war the law is dumb.'

Cicero, *Pro Milone*

The most used historical quote is possibly the opening of Psalm 46: 'God is our hope and strength, a very present help in trouble.'

Variations of these words, or very similar sentiments, have been voiced by frightened soldiers – and not a few civilians – for over 4,000 years. It makes the point that, after the elemental forces of nature, it is war that most scares humanity, and rightly so. Fear has ever been the universal emotion of the battlefield. Perhaps that is why mankind over the centuries has tried to limit war and control its bloody excesses. However, when societies elect to sort out their political, social and economic problems by resorting to killing people and breaking things, in Cicero's famous quotation, *'silent enim leger inter arma'*, or, 'In [times of] war the law is dumb'.

One of the ironies of history has been the urge to try and control behaviour that is by definition almost uncontrollable. Although mankind has tried to devise 'rules' for fighting and killing one another en masse, the truth remains that war is still nothing more than legalized murder. After the horrors of the Thirty Years War, Europeans desperately sought to find laws to channel and limit the excesses of the brutal soldiery. But the French Revolution changed all that. Out went the eighteenth-century constraints of limited war, and the full horror of war to the death between whole nations and societies was gradually unleashed, to find its ultimate expression on the Eastern Front, in the indiscriminate fire-bombings of Dresden and Tokyo, and finally at Hiroshima and Nagasaki.

One effect of mankind's new ability to obliterate and destroy on an unimaginable scale has been to encourage a new phenomenon: an increased attempt to try and control war by laws. Today, certainly in the West, we now have teams of lawyers telling soldiers and generals what they can and cannot do on the battlefield. In modern warfare the law – and its all-pervasive lawyers – seem anything but dumb.

But the irony remains that, for those enemies waging their asymmetric campaigns against Western liberal democratic states, 'the law' and lawyers are the last thing they ever care about. They just want to slaughter and maim for their cause. The old Roman was right. It was ever thus. Truly the reality remains: in war – real, all-out war – 'the law' remains as dumb as ever.

WALTER ISAACSON

'As a professor, I tended to think of history as run by impersonal forces. But when you see it in practice, you see the difference personalities make.'

Henry Kissinger

Kissinger said this in a background briefing with reporters on his Middle East shuttle mission in January 1974. He was talking about Anwar Sadat and Golda Meir and others – but perhaps subconsciously also about himself.

The role that interesting personalities can play on the world stage is why I believe that biography is a worthy aspect of history.

NIGEL JONES

'History to the defeated
May say Alas, but cannot help or pardon.'

W. H. Auden

The concluding line of Auden's great poem 'Spain', written in 1937 at the height of the Spanish Civil War, has always seemed to me both an agonizing cry of despair at the injustice and heartlessness of the Universe, and an urgent call to arms – as the author intended. Auden was actually no great shakes as a political activist himself – he was indeed, as George Orwell (a rather more active Spanish combatant) witheringly said, someone who 'was always somewhere else when a bullet is fired'.

Auden went to Spain to defend the left-wing Republic against General Franco's military rising, but in the capacity of a humble ambulance driver rather than as a soldier. Even in that role he did not last more than a few weeks. But his Spanish experience, brief though it was – like that of Orwell – was enough to change him forever. The sight of churches torched by the godless Republicans unexpectedly shocked him, and brought out the dormant Christian in Auden's soul. He junked his Communism and was eventually re-converted to Anglicanism.

The poem 'Spain', written at the peak of his left-wing enthusiasm, was intended as a propagandist plea to persuade volunteers around the world to join the Communist International Brigades and fight for the Republic. It contains, along with its moving closing line, a deeply sinister phrase: 'The conscious acceptance of guilt in the necessary murder'. Once again, this drew Orwell's scorn. It could only have been written, Orwell chided, 'by someone to whom murder is at most a word'. Orwell was right, and a shamed Auden later withdrew the phrase, declaring that no murder was ever 'necessary'. But his sentiment that the passing hem of history must be seized before it flies forever, endures.

And history has a habit of reversing its final decisions. The Republic lost the Civil War, but in today's Spain it is Francoism that is defeated, dead and buried, so in the long run the Republic may be said to have won, after all. And Auden, the passionate young Communist, lived long enough to repent his youthful folly. In its infinite wisdom, history occasionally allows such second thoughts.

TERRY JONES

'And yf that olde bokes were aweye,
Yloren were of remembraunce the keye.'

Geoffrey Chaucer, Prologue to 'The Legend of Good Women'

It was puzzling over the thirty lines describing the Knight in the Prologue to the *Canterbury Tales* that drew me in to history and kindled in me some sort of awareness of politics. And the more I go into history the more I am convinced that people don't change. The same ambitious and ruthless people seek power, and have always used the same means to gain and keep power as they use today.

In 350 BCE Aristotle wrote his dissection of political power and, I must say, it still rings true to me. He distinguished between a rightful ruler and a tyrant, not by how much power they concentrated in their own hands but by the simple gauge of ascertaining in whose interests they were operating. If they operated in the interests of the people they were ruling, then they were legitimate rulers, regardless of their power. If they operated for their own interests alone, they were by definition tyrants.

I think the same holds good today. The only difference is that nowadays we no longer apply Aristotle's yardstick. We bleat about 'democracy' and yet expect our politicians to be self-serving hypocrites. Things don't move on.

History is a never-ending Russian doll. You never get to the real core truth. But we keep turning the events and the saying over and over, hoping to get closer to the centre.

And in the act of so doing, we shed a little light on what is happening in our own world. We find, for example, that the propaganda and spin put out by Henry IV have totally skewed Richard II's reputation in Henry's favour. But little by little historians are now righting that wrong. And as we do so, we can see that spin and propaganda were no different in the early fifteenth century than they are today.

Our world is the same world that we find through history.

ANTHONY JULIUS

'All of Kabbalah is complete nonsense, but the academic study of nonsense is scholarship.'

Saul Lieberman

It is said that the great Talmudist Saul Lieberman, introducing to a university audience the similarly distinguished Kabbalist Gershom Scholem, made the above remark.

Having committed several years of my scholarly life to the writing of books about anti-Semitism, I find the remark an immense consolation.

GRACE KARSKENS

'Now, in the documents surviving from the past, the social historian can find traces – occasionally vivid glimpses – of people doing things. The searching out of the meanings that such actions contained and conveyed for the participants lies at the heart of the enterprise of ethnographic history. Actions must be viewed as statements.'

Rhys Isaac, *The Transformation of Virginia 1740–1790*

Vivid glimpses – of people doing things. Sometimes, out of the millions of words you read, a phrase like this jumps out at you, triggers a heart-stopping flash of both recognition and revelation, and then stays with you always.

In *The Transformation of Virginia*, Rhys Isaac presented deeply considered, dense and intimate readings and decoding of the actions – deliberate, symbolic or unconscious – of eighteenth-century Virginians. He was saying that actions – the actions of past peoples – speak as least as loudly as words, and that if historians carefully observe what past people did, they can recover and understand their whole worlds. Actions, gestures, movements and journeys are like holograms of their times, clues to the ways people were thinking, what mattered to them, how their cultures were constructed, and the social and physical worlds in which they moved. Of course, watching people's actions naturally leads us to examine their environments, places they made, the structures they built and the objects they used, so we can see all of these in a new light too. And it is obvious that the actions of the poor, the oppressed and outcast groups in society are just as important as those of the wealthy, powerful and literate.

My own writing on early Sydney has been inspired and guided by Rhys Isaac's work. Sydney was one of the best-documented colonies ever founded, so those 'vivid glimpses of people doing things' abound. Watching the actions of governors, convicts, bushrangers, women and Aboriginal people was a key to telling a whole new story about the origins of modern Australia.

IAN KERSHAW

*'Even though large tracts of Europe and many old and famous
States have fallen or may fall into the grip of the Gestapo and
all the odious apparatus of Nazi rule, we shall not flag or fail.
We shall go on to the end, we shall fight in France, we shall fight
on the seas and oceans, we shall fight with growing confidence
and growing strength in the air, we shall defend our island,
whatever the cost may be, we shall fight on the beaches,
we shall fight on the landing grounds, we shall fight in the
fields and in the streets, we shall fight in the hills;
we shall never surrender . . .'*

Winston Churchill

My favourite quotation from history would, I think, have to be drawn from
Winston Churchill's defiant speech to the House of Commons on 4 June
1940. He perhaps made better speeches. And other quotations from his
speeches and writings are at least as memorable – not least his 'Finest Hour'
speech a fortnight later. But I would choose this passage because of its
rhetorical importance at such a crucial moment, its morale-boosting
significance at perhaps the bleakest moment in Britain's long history.

Churchill had been Prime Minister for less than a month at the time of
the speech. His later, well-founded reputation as Britain's war hero had yet
to be established. He had come to office, on 10 May 1940, on precisely the
date that Hitler had launched his western offensive. Between that date and
the date of his speech, Churchill had to face the prospect, then certainty,
of the collapse of France and, with that, German domination of western
Europe, with the likelihood of invasion of Great Britain to follow. He had
also to surmount the arguments, articulated mainly by Lord Halifax, the
Foreign Secretary, for three days towards the end of May, that Britain
should entertain the possibility of a negotiated peace. The backcloth to the
dramatic Cabinet meetings of those days was the plight of the British
Expeditionary Force in France, penned in around Dunkirk and presumed
largely lost. Churchill himself thought perhaps only 20,000 or 30,000 could
be saved. Churchill's adamant stance that Britain should fight on whatever
happened in France finally carried the day in the Cabinet debates. And, in
what Churchill called 'the miracle of Dunkirk', almost 340,000 British and
Allied soldiers were rescued from German captivity by the armada of
vessels, many of them small fishing boats, that crossed the Channel in

perilous conditions to take the men off the beaches. It was in this context that Churchill spoke on 4 June to address the House of Commons. Though he emphasized that 'wars are not won by evacuations', he nevertheless claimed that 'there was a victory inside this deliverance'. In reality, it was a major defeat. But Churchill's rhetoric turned it into a triumph. It was a speech that helped cement Churchill's image as the indomitable war-leader needed by his country at such a dangerous time. And it did much to bolster a mood of national defiance when the situation could hardly have been more dire.

ROBERT J. KERSHAW

'Dwell on the past and you'll lose an eye.
Forget the past and you'll lose two eyes.'

Old Russian saying, quoted by Aleksandr Solzhenitsyn
in *The Gulag Archipelago*

Parachute soldiers with whom I served were taught regimental history according to the maxim 'you will never know where you are going unless you know where you came from'. We lived in a rapidly changing world where, professionally, new technologies and methods had to be quickly assimilated to retain a battle-winning edge. The past was an anchor point, providing a stable frame of reference as we innovated to branch out and deal with new issues and problems. It is criminal to shed blood when, as is often the case, there is a tendency to re-invent the wheel between generations.

But as Solzhenitsyn suggests, a degree of balance is required to view the past, which is lost if you do not.

While serving on operations I maintained a diary, recording everything seen, heard, or perceived. These were honest and frank observations, studiously ignoring security implications because there was no intent to publish in my lifetime. Perception, I realized, often fed by rumour, has the same impact as facts in producing behavioural change. Writing these diaries was later to prove invaluable, enabling me quickly to identify the authentic when researching personal historical wartime accounts, letters and diaries. The significant stood out, reflecting behaviour I instinctively knew to be true. As a consequence, when writing military history I seek sources as near as possible to the event I am examining, reconstructing scenes fed by what only the protagonists can have known or heard about. This is combined with walking the ground, using the maps available at the time, alongside eye-witness testimony, to recreate the scene. These are the two eyes that the Russian saying encourages us to use, not the eye-patch perspective that an unquestioning acceptance of secondary sources might bring.

JIM AL-KHALILI

*'The seeker after truth is not one who studies the writings of the
ancients and, following his natural disposition, puts his trust
in them, but rather the one who suspects his faith in them and
questions what he gathers from them, the one who submits to
argument and demonstration and not the sayings of human
beings whose nature is fraught with all kinds of imperfection
and deficiency. Thus the duty of the man who investigates the
writings of scientists, if learning the truth is his goal, is to make
himself an enemy of all that he reads, and, applying his mind
to the core and margins of its content, attack it from every side.
He should also suspect himself as he performs his critical
examination of it, so that he may avoid falling into
either prejudice or leniency.'*

Al-Hasan Ibn al-Haytham, *Doubts on Ptolemy*

Ibn al-Haytham (Latinized as Alhazen) was an Arab scientist and one of
the most remarkable scholars of medieval times. I regard him not only as
the greatest physicist of the 2,000-year span between Archimedes and
Newton, but one of the earliest proponents of the scientific method. He
made many contributions in the fields of optics and astronomy. His *Book
of Optics* had a huge influence on the development of Western science. He
is often referred to as the 'first true scientist'. He was the first to explain
correctly how vision works in terms of geometric optics and made advances
in 'mathematizing' astronomy and wrote on celestial mechanics.

In this quote, he shows clearly that he was one of the founders of a
movement known as the *shukuk* ('doubts'), which advocated the critical
analysis of the scientific legacy of past masters, most notably the great
Greek scholars such as Aristotle and the astronomer Ptolemy, whose work
was translated into Arabic during the ninth and tenth centuries CE. Ibn al-
Haytham stresses that one should not accept the word of these men without
question, but should always have doubts over the validity of their ideas and
theories.

And that is of course how science works today, and this is what his
comment that 'one should make himself the enemy of all that he reads'
implies.

HENRY KISSINGER

'There cannot be a crisis next week.
My schedule is already full.'

'The great tragedies of history occur not when
right confronts wrong but when two rights
confront each other.'

'History knows no resting place and no plateaus.'

With thanks to Dr Henry Kissinger for granting permission to use the above quotations.

IAN KNIGHT

'First comes the trader. Then the missionary.
Then, the Red Soldier.'

Cetshwayo kaMpande, *c.* 1878

During the latter part of 1878, the Zulu king, Cetshwayo kaMpande, felt himself under threat from increasingly hostile neighbours. In 1824 his predecessor, the famous King Shaka, had allowed a small, bedraggled group of shipwrecked British adventurers a toe-hold on the shores of a natural lagoon, known to the outside world as Port Natal, which lay on the southern fringes of Zulu influence. In the fifty years since, the British had annexed the lagoon's hinterland as the colony of Natal, and that first ramshackle camp had become the town of Durban. Inland, to the west, the Zulu kingdom had found itself hemmed in, too, by the Transvaal Republic, founded by Boer settlers who had moved north from the Cape.

For half a century, the Zulu kings had enjoyed a good relationship with their British neighbours – and a rather more problematic one with the Transvaal – but during the 1870s a change of outlook in the Colonial Office in far-away London had seen the British adopt a new, aggressive policy in southern Africa. In 1877 Britain had annexed the Transvaal, and King Cetshwayo's initial relief turned to unease as he noted an increasingly confrontational tone in his dealings with the British – and slowly began to realize that his Zulu kingdom now stood in the way of Imperial expansion.

There was, he recognized, a distinct paradigm to British progress across the region. First came those who were tempted by the profits to be had when a new African society was first opened up to European penetration; then, as, the British presence became more settled, followed those who wanted to save souls and civilize. By which time, he realized, most African groups had glimpsed the looming danger, and many had opted to resist – with only one sure result. It was an uncannily accurate prediction of the Zulus' fate; in 1848 an Irish trader named James Rorke had bought a large farm on the borders of Natal and Zululand, and traded across the dividing river by a ford which became known as Rorke's Drift. In 1877 the farm had passed to the Swedish Mission Society, and a missionary named Otto Witt had bought it. And, as King Cetshwayo found himself steadily manipulated into a confrontation with his British neighbours, so, in January 1879, Lieutenant General Lord Chelmsford led a column of British redcoats across the border to invade Zululand from Rorke's Drift.

PHILLIP KNIGHTLEY

Voting 'No'.

Historians are always searching for an event that goes beyond its obvious significance and illuminates a wider perspective. In my book *Australia: A Biography of a Nation* I found one such event that made several telling points. During the First World War, because of heavy casualties and a lack of volunteers, the Australian government decided conscription was the answer and held a referendum on the issue. Most Anglo-Australians supported the government. Most Irish-Australians opposed it. It split the nation and the 'No' vote had a small majority.

But that was not the end of the matter. There was a mutiny in the Army when 15,000 troops refused to accept an increase of one and a half hours in their daily training, and then a general strike which threatened food supplies. The Prime Minister, William Hughes, could not believe that Australians could be so disloyal when Australian servicemen were dying overseas and Britain was fighting for its life on the battlefields of France. He wanted Australia to have even closer ties to Britain and surrender some of its independence to an 'Empire Parliament' which would have Australian representatives. He thought that, given a second chance to express their devotion to Britain, Australians would vote 'Yes' for conscription and 'Yes' for King and Empire. He was wrong.

This time an even larger majority voted against conscription and, in a telling blow to the government, almost half of the soldiers at the front voted 'No'. These two anti-conscription referendums had wider significance. They forced Australians to think about their attitudes to nationalism and their bond to Britain and they highlighted for liberal intellectuals the conservatism of the Australian middle class. They also proved the power of the Australian sense of fairness and personal liberty – if a man wanted to go overseas and fight, then that was his business, but no one had the right to force him to do so.

GUIDO KNOPP

'From time to time, history loves to become condensed in one person all at once, whom the whole world then obeys.'

Jacob Burckhardt

The Third Reich was not conceivable without him: Hitler was the centre of evil, his delusion threatened to rule the world. Himself being a product of history he made history in a way that was without paradigm. He was the worst-case scenario in German history.

And still there has been no answer to the question how a scruffy under-dog like him could take over the power in a civilized society. Jacob Burckhardt's phrase points to the inner mechanism of history, to the enigma of history, to the human factor in history. Whatever we know about history – these three aspects we will never fully understand – nor will we be able to control them.

ANDREW LAMBERT

'History is a record of exploded ideas!'

Admiral Sir John Fisher

Between 1899 and 1902 Fisher, later Lord Fisher of Kilverstone, was the Commander-in-Chief of the British Mediterranean Fleet. The quote was a typical bravura statement deployed in a lecture given to senior officers under his command. He went on to develop the theme that the conditions of modern naval warfare with armoured steamships, mines and torpedoes had fundamentally altered the nature of war and that under these circumstances he would be the directing intellect of any campaign or battle.

In truth Fisher's purpose was less obvious. Throughout his Mediterranean command he was at loggerheads with the Admiralty over the size of his fleet. The Admiralty case, largely developed by Rear Admiral Reginald Custance, the Director of Naval Intelligence, depended on historical examples from the age of Nelson. Consequently, Fisher's line, far from being a critique of history, or of Nelson, was intended to discredit Custance's use of the past. Fisher, who idolized Nelson, would do more to exploit the intellectual value of history for serving officers than any other First Sea Lord.

Sir Julian Corbett, the greatest naval historian, worked closely with Fisher in and out of office for more than a decade, educating senior officers and developing national strategy through historical research. Fisher's views were clear: any history used to attack his policies was indeed 'a record of exploded ideas', but any examples he chose carried enormous weight.

It all depends on the context.

PAUL LAY

'History is a great deal closer to poetry than is generally realized; in truth, I think, it is in essence the same.'

A. L. Rowse

There is one aspect of the practice of history that is increasingly forgotten, especially in its teaching: communication. A. L. Rowse, that cantankerous mixture of internal conflict, ego and elegance, always sought the widest possible audience and gained it through his often controversial, sometimes outlandish studies of Elizabethan England. Much of his ability to communicate came from his skill as a poet, a lifelong passion. It enabled him to turn the perfect phrase, craft his precise prose to perfection, carry his audience with him. In that, he was the forerunner of the best narrative historians of our own time, not least, David Starkey, similarly combative, humble of birth, an original and a showman who believes that history should be available to all who seek it, that it's much too important a subject to leave to historians alone.

This theme of history as poetry – distilled, intense, dramatic and true – is shared by others. Mark Twain wrote that: 'The past does not repeat itself, but it rhymes.' The great scholar of the Renaissance Jacob Burckhardt considered history as 'still in large measure poetry to me'. They, like Rowse, understood that the best history must be communicated to the widest possible audience. As editor of *History Today* I know that it is a rare gift.

QUENTIN LETTS

'A day like today is not a day for soundbites, we can leave those at home. But I feel the hand of history upon our shoulder with respect to this, I really do.'

Tony Blair

Tony Blair was nearing his first anniversary as British prime minister when he made his 'hand of history' remark at the start of talks which led to the Good Friday Agreement. The deal led to the reopening of the Stormont Assembly, formalizing Sinn Féin's disavowal of violence.

Mr Blair's remark was a collector's item for several reasons. One we easily overlook today is that it was one of the first times the political sound-bite became so laughably obvious. Even the most trusting of voters was able to look at Blair's remark and see that he was clumsily trying to get himself on the newspaper front pages. The British public was slowly waking up to Mr Blair as a show pony. This quotation helped that process and allowed us to laugh at a man who until this point had been under-mocked.

Mr Blair's aide, Jonathan Powell, has said that the prime minister did not pre-cook his remark. This is testament to Mr Blair's gifts as a communicator. 'Hand of history' is a striking image, redolent of a great Biblical hand reaching down from the heavens. Was it Mr Blair's interest in scripture which germinated the idea? Or was it something more like the digits which would appear through the clouds in Monty Python? Although there is nothing strictly religious in the remark, it is hard to imagine a secular politician producing such a spontaneous phrase.

He said it at the start of arduous talks which lasted many hours. The remark, broadcast live that night on television, created pressure on the other participants. It also – typical Blair – placed its creator at the very centre of the negotiations, even though they were arguably more the business of Ireland's politicians, north and south. Mr Blair was presenting himself to us as the agent of an almost divine fate. Other British prime ministers, chiefly Margaret Thatcher and John Major, had taken greater risks on Northern Ireland but Tony Blair was the one trying to scoop the credit. To some extent he succeeded.

Looking back, who is to say that the Good Friday talks were not momentous? Despite the vanity and self-interest which lay behind it, the Blair quotation was to some extent true. That is what sets it apart from the merely absurd and makes it one of the defining quotations of the New Labour era. Show pony or not, Mr Blair had a knack for being in interesting places at interesting times. He would have made a good TV foreign correspondent.

LEANDA DE LISLE

'Science and technology revolutionize our lives, but memory, tradition and myth frame our response. Expelled from individual consciousness by the rush of change, history finds its revenge by stamping the collective unconscious with habits, values, expectations, dreams.'

Arthur M. Schlesinger Jr.

The frightening thing about deep-rooted prejudices is that those who express them are so often unaware of what they are doing. They see themselves as 'modern' and 'secular' and therefore rational and compassionate, never questioning deeply the basis of their beliefs, or the logic. In describing and telling the stories of the past, historians hold a mirror to the present. We can see ourselves from unexpected angles, and what we see may act as a spur, or a check. Often, however, the writing of history has simply flattered the powerful. The fact that, historically, there have been fewer women writers of history has deprived us of the viewpoint of the institutionally weaker sex. I am not sure what difference my gender makes to my writing today, but I suspect it colours my interest in the changing ways in which we have justified the power of some groups over others, and the urge to dehumanise the weakest amongst us.

If I was going to choose my favourite quote from history rather than about history it would be from Demosthenes: 'The easiest thing of all is to deceive oneself; for what a man wishes he generally believes to be true.'

Historians should help give us perspective, and some insight into our unconscious: the truth is not convenient.

JOHN LUKACS

'History is not made by documents. Documents are made by history.'

'History does not consist of "facts". It is written, taught, spoken, thought in words. Its facts are inseparable from the words in which they are stated. Words have their own histories, too: their lives and deaths, their powers and their limits. Let us imagine (it is not easy, but imaginable) that at some future time people may communicate with each other entirely by pictures, images, numbers, even the peoples' consciousness of history, including their own history, will continue to exist.'

'The purpose of historians is NOT the definite establishment of truths. It is the correction and the elimination of untruths and half truths.'

'There was this old Irish biddy whom the neighbours asked, whether the gossip about the young widow up the street was true? She said: "It is not true; but it is true enough." The historian must think conversely: "This may be true; but it is not true enough."'

'One trouble is that so many professional historians are less interested in history than they are in their historianship.'

'The prime question is not (or should be no longer) whether History is Art or Science. It should be: is the writing of history Science or Literature? It should be the latter.'

'The difference between a "professional" and "amateur" historian is no more than one between a professional and an amateur brain surgeon; but it is less than between a "professional" (an absurdity, isn't it?) and an "amateur" poet.'

'A celebrity is someone who is famous for being well-known. My ambition has been to be famous for not being well-known.'

ROBERT LYMAN

'However changed and strange the new conditions of war may be, not only generals, but politicians and ordinary citizens, may find there is much to be learned from the past that can be applied to the future and, in their search for it, that some campaigns have more than others foreshadowed the coming pattern of modern war. I believe that ours in Burma was one of these. This may seem a curious claim to make for the struggles of comparatively ill-equipped men, groping through jungles. Yet a painter's effect and style do not depend on how many tubes of colour he has, the number of his brushes, or the size of his canvas, but on how he blends his colours and handles his brushes against the canvas.'

Field Marshal Sir William Slim

By the time he penned these words in 1956 Field Marshal Sir William ('Bill') Slim knew that the remarkable successes of his Fourteenth Army in India in 1944, and in Burma the following year, had already been largely forgotten by a country desperate to move on from the long traumas of the Second World War, but also by military strategists intent on focusing on the small wars of imperial contraction and the lessons of armoured warfare in Europe, useful for dealing with questions of how to fight a possible war with the Warsaw Pact. These 'lessons', propagated vociferously by Montgomery of Alamein and his disciples, rubbished the experience of fighting in the Far East as a 'Sepoy's War' offering nothing in terms of historical significance compared to the great armoured confrontations in North Africa, northern Europe and the Soviet steppes. Not one to blow his own trumpet, Slim merely noted the reality that history was often dictated by those who made the most sound.

Yet, in his claim that Burma provided a remarkably apt template for the study of modern warfare he was to be proved right, but not until long after his own demise. Despite the fact that its resources, compared to British armies fighting in Italy and Europe, had been severely constrained, Slim's Fourteenth Army created an entirely new approach to warfare, for the British at least, which can be described as being akin to 'manoeuvre of the mind'. At the heart of this doctrine is the notion that the art of strategy is to undermine an enemy's mental strengths and his will to win, through the concentration of force to achieve surprise, psychological shock, physical momentum and moral dominance. It is an approach to war that sits in stark contrast to the idea of matching strength with strength, and force with force, and where the goal of strategy is not simply to slog it out with an enemy in an attritional confrontation of the type that characterized much of British experience in North Africa and Europe. A modern commander made in Slim's mould prizes above all the virtues of cunning and guile, seeks shamelessly to trick and deceive the enemy and bases his operational plan firmly upon the ruthless exploitation of the enemy's weaknesses. Slim's approach, described by one of his divisional commanders to be like 'shooting a goal while the referee wasn't watching', depended on strong leadership at every level of command, intensive training and preparation, and the encouragement of a vigorous culture across the army that rewarded the ingenuity, boldness and the initiative of all ranks. As a consequence the Fourteenth Army became perhaps the most dynamic and successful British army to take to the field since the days of Wellington, despite the fact that it boasted a fraction of the resources that would have been considered necessary were it to deploy against the Germans in Europe.

It wasn't until the late 1980s that the real lessons for historians of warfare from the long struggles in India and Burma between 1942 and 1945, pointed to by Slim in 1956, finally began to receive the credit they were due.

It is often said that history is written by the victor. It is also true that it often only remembers the loudest drum.

GAVIN M^CLEAN

'But history differs from heritage not, as people generally suppose, in telling the truth, but in trying to do so despite being aware that truth is a chameleon and its chroniclers fallible beings. The most crucial distinction is that truth in heritage commits us to some present creed; truth in history is a flawed effort to understand the past on its own terms.'

David Lowenthal

Although I think that David Lowenthal is sometimes a little harsh on heritage and on popular history in his provocative book *The Heritage Crusade and the Spoils of History*, I like to drop this quote on my architecture, public history and museum and heritage students.

It's a stimulating bucket of cold water. The land-based historic heritage projects that many will work on are usually driven by a mix of economic, political and cultural factors. Nation- and community-building, urban regeneration, these are just some of the catch-phrases invoked as crumbling waterfronts get the makeover to take them from ship to shop(pe).

Architects, planners, politicians and property owners tend to fetishize the tangible. Often the historian is the only member in a multi-disciplinary project team interested in the past for its own sake. So they have to understand these tensions, put intangible values alongside aesthetics and argue for the themes and periods others may overlook or prefer to avoid.

There's nothing wrong with community pride, but I think that we need curmudgeons as well as cheerleaders.

FRANK M^CLYNN

*'On the shore where time casts up its stray wreckage,
we gather corks and broken planks, whence much
indeed may be argued and more guessed; but what
the great ship was that has gone down into the deep,
that we shall never see.'*

G. M.Trevelyan

The historian has to work with scraps, an archive here, a memoir there, even oral history. The written record available is a tiny part of the real past, what some have called (using another watery image) the historical deposit, the lees left behind when the waters of time recede. The difficulties multiply, because official archives are always tendentious, usually designed to place a government or a minister in a good light. This is why the best historical records are the 'incidental' ones – rent rolls, customs returns, census figures – albeit the driest.

It is an elementary fallacy to imagine that one can reconstruct history from archives alone, though we do not have to go all the way with H. L. Mencken, who described the historian as an unsuccessful novelist. Too much has perhaps been made of the element of 'guesswork' involved in interpreting the past. There are dud conjectures and inspired and brilliant ones, which make sense of the fragments at our disposal.

The great historian must go behind the archives and intuit the historical totality, which is why all the most famous 'theses', by Pirenne, Turner, A. J. P. Taylor, *et al.* are always controversial.

HUGH MᶜMANNERS

'The past is a foreign country: they do things differently there.'

L. P. Hartley, *The Go-Between*

The historian's job is to narrate in order to explain the events of the past in two ways: in relation to other events creating a broad sweep of history eventually to the present day; but also in relation to the present, and how those events, people and actions can be compared with what we do in the present. But, for me, history's most important and interesting value lies in explaining how people separated by just a few generations can behave in ways that seem extraordinary to us today.

Ethnography uses what is referred to as the 'ethnographic present tense' to allow, for example, the 'potlatch' feasting and entertaining of neighbours by hunter-gather tribes of North America's Pacific Northwest to be compared directly with the show-partying of Wall Street financiers. The similarities are striking.

My father, the late John McManners, who was Regius Professor of Ecclesiastical History at Oxford, explained in one particularly vivid chapter of his *Death in the Enlightenment*, how cultured, decent people could attend the deliberately cruel public executions through which law and order were maintained in that era. Many admitted to looking away at critical moments, but felt it their civic duty to attend in support of the rule of law, with chaos lurking in the shadows.

I do, however, draw my own personal line at the habit of some historians to speak of their period of expertise in the present tense, as if they were so familiar with it as to be unable to distinguish it from reality. For me, this differentiation is vital; history unrelated to the present is story-telling – entertainment. Furthermore, in talking of the past in the present tense, one misrepresents it as if a costume drama with modern players, but worse – as if those events have had no effect on events thereafter and so the future from which you are commenting.

The past is a foreign country, where, if only because they have not yet experienced our past, they very certainly do things very differently. This is the very essence of history – remembering the past, lest we condemn ourselves to repeat it.

Spanish philosopher and writer George Santayana, whom I have paraphrased here, was equally sound on war and liberalism: 'Only the dead have seen the end of war.'

ALLAN MALLINSON

'Armies do not win wars by means of a few bodies of super-soldiers but by the average quality of their standard units.'

Field Marshal Sir William Slim, *Defeat Into Victory*

Slim was reflecting on the opportunity cost of the Chindit operations in Burma, which had taken many high-quality men from workaday units, and cautioning against any similar tendency in the future, though he recognized the need for Special Forces.

The British Army's success over the years has lain in just this maxim: that it is the high average quality of the 'standard units' – predominantly the infantry – which counts. Notwithstanding the performance of the more elite airborne forces at Arnhem and in the Falklands, time and again it has been the regiments of the line – sometimes even the most 'unfashionable' – that have pulled off those feats of arms which stand so high in the estimation of other armies.

There was nothing 'elite' about the Glosters, for example, at the Imjin River in Korea; nor the Suffolks in Malaya, who killed more insurgents than any other regiment; nor the Princess of Wales's Royal Regiment in Iraq, with all their decorations for resource and bravery, including the VC. The British Army, in its 350 years of continuous existence, has by the deeds of its individual regiments kept raising the bar of 'average quality'. And this is why it can sometimes be said to punch above its weight today.

JOHN MAN

'A historian who would convey the truth must lie.'

Mark Twain

Mark Twain's paradox goes to the heart of what historians do.

History is three things: what happened; the records of what happened; and what we do with the records to explain ourselves to ourselves. Unless we are malign control freaks – dictators, fanatics – we aim to capture truth. This is impossible, because the past is infinite and obscure. All we poor humans can do is select and distill, hoping to read the universe by snatching at grains of dust.

From these grains we make stories. If the stories are good, if the words and images are chosen with flair and good intent, they give the impression of being true. That is the magic of good historical writing, good films, good documentaries, whatever. It's an illusion, created by selecting snippets and ignoring all the rest. There is no truth in history, only countless attempts to tell it.

We are the product of infinite, unreachable complexity, and our only hope is to aim for truth by telling our lies with good intentions, generation after generation.

HILARY MANTEL

*'I am seeking to rescue the poor stockinger,
the Luddite cropper, the "obsolete" hand-loom
weaver, the "utopian" artisan, and even the deluded
follower of Joanna Southcott, from the enormous
condescension of posterity.'*

E. P. Thompson

When E. P. Thompson wrote this in the preface to his groundbreaking 1963 book *The Making of the English Working Class*, this most English of historians was telling us that we should consider our working forefathers and mothers as much a part of history as generals, politicians, theologians and artists. Working people, whose history often lies between the lines of the orthodox account, should not be viewed as victims, as statistical units, or mere tools of economic development; they are worthy of our respectful consideration, and we should be alive to the efforts they made to take charge of their own destinies.

But there is a more general point. Every working historian and commentator, whatever his or her field, needs to check at every turn: am I guilty of 'enormous condescension' towards the dead? People in the past had a different world view from ours. They did not know what we know, but they knew things we have forgotten. Education was less general, but native wit was never in short supply. Lives were shorter, but the lost were no less deeply mourned. If we pity them as superstitious, they might pity us for lacking curiosity or a sense of the strangeness of the world. Hindsight suggests what they could have done, should have done, but they did not have the advantage of hindsight; like us, they were walking forward into the dark. They may be dead, but they are our equals, and if we respect them we can learn from them.

JUSTIN MAROZZI

'Herodotus of Halicarnassus here displays his inquiry,
so that human achievements may not become forgotten
in time, and great and marvellous deeds – some
displayed by Greeks, some by barbarians – may not
be without their glory; and especially to show why
the two peoples fought each other.'

Herodotus, *Histories*

There it is. The birth of history in a paragraph. Herodotus must take pride of place in any historical anthology. With these few words, written in the fifth century BCE, the Greek Father of History first formulates humankind's burning interest in the past, an obsession that has remained with us ever since. His mission, as noble as it is ambitious, is to record and explain what has been before, to ensure that glorious achievements and remarkable events are preserved in memory and not forgotten, to make sense of the cataclysm of the Persian Wars and try to understand why the weaker side won and the more powerful lost, to examine, through his travels and on-the-road researches, the clash of cultures and customs between the Greek and barbarian worlds. Technically history will come later, but it will come from the Greek word Herodotus uses here: ιστορίη or *historie*, inquiry or investigation.

Herodotus is compulsively readable 2,500 years after he wrote the world's first history book. I took him to war in Iraq in 2004 and he proved the perfect historical guide to another seismic conflict pitting East against West, an echo of the Persian Wars he chronicled so carefully and with such élan.

If the quote above is a due recognition of Herodotus as the Father of History, his wisdom and humanity are confirmed in his timeless observation about the tragedy of human conflict: 'No one is fool enough to choose war instead of peace – in peace sons bury fathers but in war fathers bury sons.'

MICHAEL R. MARRUS

'Whatever it is that the law is after, it is not the whole story.'

Clifford Geertz, *Local Knowledge: Further Essays in Interpretative Anthropology*

Recently, I have been interested in the relationship between law and history. Pondering these two approaches to evaluations of the past, I return often to the wise comment of the anthropologist Clifford Geertz, who had as fine an eye as any to the scope of each discipline when it came to the past.

Law, Geertz understood, has not functioned well, particularly in countries ruled by the common law, when it comes to getting to the bottom of an issue – what we usually mean when we refer loosely to the 'whole story'. Over many years the law has evolved in order to reach judgments that can be practically administered, sustain the values of society, and are fair. These are eminently worthy objectives, part of what we call the Rule of Law.

The law's objectives differ in two important respects from the work of historians. First, what the law is primarily after is the resolution of disputes, defined by courts and arrived at through well-established procedures. Second, courts reach such resolutions through argument and the presentation of evidence, the admissibility of which is defined by rules that have evolved over centuries and are designed, among other things, to protect defendants. Context, the life blood of historians, which makes histories come alive and sometimes persuades, is often deemed irrelevant or prejudicial. Historians, by contrast, pursue whatever questions they like and provide evidence that they find persuasive or simply interesting. For the law, established institutions issue judgments, operating according to well-defined procedures; for historians, there are many ways to talk about the past, and when questions are raised it is the readers who ultimately provide the answers.

CHARLES MESSENGER

*'What experience and history teach is this – that people
and governments never have learnt anything from
history, or have acted on principles deduced from it.'*

Georg Wilhelm Friedrich Hegel

The German philosopher Hegel argued that reason and reality are identical
and that reality is represented by facts that appear as state, art, religion and
history. He lived through a tumultuous period of history, notably the
Revolutionary and Napoleonic Wars which swept to and fro across Europe.
It was perhaps with this in mind that he made this apt observation, which
is just as applicable to today's world.

History is filled with politicians who have failed to draw on the lessons
of the past. Indeed their policies have often been merely reinventions of
the wheel. The same has applied to the military, at least the victors of
previous wars. They have often been content to rest on their laurels and
fight the next war as they did the last, while the vanquished do learn the
lessons and reap the benefit from them. Perhaps even more apposite to
today's world is recognition that history is littered with examples of the
unexpected occurring, especially in the context of framing foreign and
defence policy.

ALEXANDER MIKABERIDZE

'There are two kinds of men: the ones who make history and the ones who endure it.'

Camilo José Cela

Popular history tends to concentrate on great men of history and their actions, oftentimes portrayed as heroic and worthy of adulation, that shaped the course of their country or people. Yet, in this emphasis on the great men who 'made' that history, we oftentimes forget those ordinary men who have 'endured' it in the process. As a military historian, I am particularly interested in human experiences of battle. For many, military history is the study of generals and generalship. But it is one thing to discuss the military campaigns of Napoleon, Alexander of Macedon or Gustavus Adolphus and ponder on their generalship. Yet it is quite different to delve deeper into the human experiences that accompanied these historical events. History must not only deal with the great events of the era but has to discuss also how those events shaped the mental and emotional lives of the people who lived through them.

It is not enough for me to understand how military institutions evolved, what motivated commanders to make particular decisions, or how the battle's course unfolded throughout a day. I am equally interested in how ordinary soldiers were affected by such decisions, how they lived through the events of that day or what motivated them to act the way they did. Thus, in my writings I seek to explain what guided those famous *pontoniers* of the Grande Armée who stood in the frozen waters of the Berezina building the bridges on which the army escaped the Russian wrath; or what ordinary soldiers felt or experienced as they waited in their bivouacs on the eve of a decisive battle. Such micro-historical analysis only enriches history and allows us a better understanding of the past.

DAN MILLS

*'I am the punishment of God, if you had not
committed great sins God would not have sent
a punishment like me upon you.'*

Genghis Khan

I have always been very interested in history, in particular military history. This particular quote is from the thirteenth century and comes from one of history's most formidable military leaders, Genghis Khan; it is about revenge.

It is believed Genghis said this after the massacre of 150,000 inhabitants during his 1221 siege and battle of 'The White City', in Bamiyan Valley. Thus the city became known as 'The City of Screams' (Shahr-i-Gholghola), and still is today almost eight centuries later.

The entire valley was razed to the ground in revenge for the loss of the Great Khan's favourite grandson during the battle. So furious was Genghis it was reported that he even had all the mice killed!

Genghis Khan was born Temujin *c.* 1162 and died in 1227 at approximately sixty-five years old. It is believed he was born with a blood clot grasped in his clenched hand, a sign that he was to become a great leader.

After uniting the Mongol clans on the plains of north-east Asia he went on to conquer most of Eurasia. By the time of his death the Mongol empire covered large tracts of Central Asia and China and he was credited as being the founding father of Mongolia.

I was interested in the quote not only because it provokes thought, but also because I had earlier read that he was most likely a shaman, and therefore wondered which 'God' he spoke of. Religion has for centuries been the cause of war, though he would have to have been most confident and deeply devoted to the god he worshipped to make such a statement. In fact it is known that he was tolerant of other religions, often taking the opportunity to consult Buddhist monks, Muslim traders on the Silk Road, and Christian missions, ever aware of the need for alliances and knowledge.

CHRISTOPHER MOORE

'Today Catharism is no more than a dead star, whose cold but fascinating light reaches us now after an eclipse of more than half a millennium. But Montaillou itself is much more than a courageous but fleeting deviation. It is the factual history of ordinary people. It is Pierre and Beatrice and their love; it is Pierre Maury and his flock. It is the breath of life restored through a repressive Latin register that is a monument of Occitan literature. Montaillou is the physical warmth of the ostal, together with the ever-recurring promise of a peasant heaven. The one within the other, the one supporting the other.'

Emmanuel Le Roy Ladurie, *Montaillou: The Promised Land of Error*

In the late 1970s, I was trying to write about the lives of ordinary people in eighteenth-century French Canada. A friend in France recommended *Montaillou*, Le Roy Ladurie's recently published and very popular study of one small village in the Pyrenees around the year 1300. I discovered *Montaillou* as at once a thick, difficult text in austere French and the best history book I had ever read. I slowly, slowly worked my way through, learning of a whole village incarcerated for heresy, and of the meticulous transcript of the villagers' testimony that in his hands became the most vivid account of medieval peasant experience ever written.

I finished *Montaillou* feeling moved and inspired and imagining myself about the only person in English-speaking North America who knew this story. Then I picked up *Time* magazine in a supermarket checkout line and read a review of the new English translation, just published in paperback and destined for bestseller lists around the world.

Much from *Montaillou* stays with me, but particularly that image of history as light from dead stars. It remains the most vivid image I know of history's gifts to us. It is a romantic image, to be sure. History as physical warmth. History as the breath of life. History as love. A dangerous image, too, for we should know historical sources are always shaped by the teller, by the circumstances that produced the testimony, by the hazards that preserved it for us. Historical evidence never comes pure as light.

Despite the claims of so many dust jackets, history as light from dead stars insists that nothing can make history 'come to life'. The past is truly distant, as truly vanished as a solar system gone nova long ago on the other side of the galaxy. Yet the past leaves its ambiguous trace, like the light of other days floating down across the years to make a precious, tenuous bond between past and present, between our human experience and that of our predecessors.

The image is also a testimony of conversion from Emmanuel Le Roy Ladurie. Le Roy Ladurie was one of the star historians of France's *Annales* school of *histoire économique et sociale*, with its message of commitment to the *longue durée* and its disdain for 'mere events'. Le Roy Ladurie's *Peasants of Languedoc*, indeed, deeply quantitative and statistical, is a masterwork of that school, a powerful demonstration that for peasant society in the south of France, simply nothing of true significance happened from 1400 to 1800 beyond the working out of a long, slow, inexorable agrarian cycle.

As a historical apprentice, then, I aspired to that kind of seriousness. But I wanted what *Montaillou* promises too, the breath of life, the glimpse of humanity. Still do. The one and the other.

ROGER MOORHOUSE

'You may pronounce us guilty a thousand times over but the goddess of the eternal court of history will smile and tear to tatters the sentence of this court. For she acquits us.'

Adolf Hitler

In the spring of 1924, Adolf Hitler stood trial in Munich for high treason for his leading role in the Nazi attempt to seize power the previous autumn. Standing in his black tails, with his toothbrush moustache and slicked hair, he cut a curious figure alongside the bemedalled ex-soldiers who stood arraigned with him.

Many watching the court proceedings of that spring assumed that the trial would be the end of Hitler, that he would prove to be a footnote in history, a political failure soon to rank alongside the countless other cranks, crackpots and failed revolutionaries that litter European history. *The Times* of London, for instance, haughtily (and erroneously) dismissed him as a 'house-painter and demagogue', whilst the author Stefan Zweig opined that Hitler had fallen back 'into oblivion'. Such sentiments would only have been strengthened by the court's verdict, which sentenced Hitler to five years' detention in the fortress-prison of Landsberg.

In his final speech to the court, Hitler was predictably unrepentant. He goaded his prosecutors, rejecting their verdict and telling them that he considered himself subject to another, higher power. For all his bluster, Hitler was duly sent to prison. Though he only served eight months of his five-year sentence before being pardoned, when he emerged he found himself again confined to the wilder fringes of German political life. It was only the eruption of the economic crisis in 1929 that rescued his career, and thrust him once again into the spotlight. The rest – as they say – is history.

Historians naturally seek to make sense of the past; to package it, rationalize it and present it in a comprehensible form. Yet, despite our best efforts, we are reminded at every turn that history – like human life itself – often has more than a whiff of caprice, randomness and chaos about it. To paraphrase another revolutionary – Lenin – 'it is not by straight lines that history proceeds, but by zig-zags and roundabout ways'.

Few would have believed, that day in the spring of 1924, that Adolf Hitler – the odious demagogue of the Munich Putsch Trial – was the coming man of Germany. But the 'goddess of history', it seems, had other ideas.

MELISSA MÜLLER

'I don't believe that the big men, the politicians and the
capitalists alone, are responsible for the war. Oh no, the little
man is just as guilty, otherwise the peoples of the world would
have risen in revolt long ago! There's in people simply an urge
to destroy, an urge to kill, to murder and rage, and until all
mankind, without exception, undergoes a great change, wars
will be waged, everything that has been built up, cultivated,
and grown will be disfigured and destroyed after which
mankind will have to begin all over again.'

Anne Frank, 3 May 1944

Otto Frank only realized that 'his girl' was a critical independent-thinking young woman when he read Anne's diary. He emphasized this in many interviews. He had underestimated his daughter – like so many parents who underestimate their developing children.

Anne was just two months away from her fifteenth birthday when she gave vent to her anger about people's indifference. She had been confined to her hiding-place in Amsterdam's Prinsengracht for twenty-two months – cut off from the outside world, condemned to passivity, surrounded by her family and yet so alone. Fear and desperation were her daily companions, teenagers' dreams an occasional consolation. In such a difficult situation many succumb to self-pity – but not Anne.

She scrutinized herself and simultaneously matured in fast-motion. She fought – against the usual roles of parents and children, but above all with herself – for independent thought, and discovered she had a will of her own. She consequently rubbed people up the wrong way and constantly came into conflict with the adult world looking down on her, but she allowed herself to stay strong and to form her own opinions.

The Nazis and their silent helpers could take Anne's life from her but could not silence her voice, which still rings out for all of us, whom she had hoped so ardently to serve. 'If God lets me live . . . I shall not remain insignificant, I shall work in the world for mankind,' she resolved. To say 'Yes' if she was convinced of the cause, and to insist on her 'No' when necessary loudly and audibly.

Does one have to be a hero to indulge in such freedom? If only conforming wasn't so much easier.

BILL NASSON

'*The hearse of history is not far from the playground, and the subject is already half dead.*'

Charles Van Onselen

This is a characteristically pungent comment by South Africa's pre-eminent living historian, Charles Van Onselen. Made well over a decade ago, in 1997, it was directed at the mouldy state of history in South African society and the grave-digger role of its own professional historians. If it was relevant then, Professor Van Onselen's barb is, if anything, more relevant now, and not only for his own society. It may even provide sobering food for thought for some beyond the Witwatersrand and the Cape of Good Hope.

Part of the general point being made about history's funereal condition was a context of unexpected vulnerability. With the crumbling of Afrikaner nationalism and the end of white minority rule, hopes in education were high that historical knowledge would be reinvigorated. One impulse was the capacity of a newly inclusive history to fuel a shared national memory. Another was the need to provide a common citizenry with a critical grasp of historical knowledge. Yet such optimism turned out to be misconceived. With its disciplinary stature increasingly diluted, history in schools was withering into the cuckoo-rearing nests of integrated social studies. In effect, the historical past was almost invariably becoming either the present or, at best, the near present.

No less – indeed, perhaps more – dispiriting than the recognition of an educational corpse at the school gate is the second part of the notion of history being eroded. That is the way in which professional historians have become implicated in its demise. Instead of touching or trying to touch the imagination of a general reading public as some earlier historians of South Africa once sought to do, the country's professional history writers have mostly withdrawn from any common conversation with an everyday audience. In an exchange of numbingly dry products or fields, historians write for each other, no longer trading a literary craft of good writing.

For non-fiction to regain life amidst ordinary people, scholarship needs to dip into the ancestral richness of literary narrative so that it, too, cultivates the classic idioms of human experience like irony, malice and calamity. South Africa's divided past has its fair share of those. In illum-inating its complexities, the power of history can challenge the more unreasoning forces which stalk the present.

TIM NEWARK

'While only a foolish Conservative would judge the present by the standards of the past, only a foolish Liberal would judge the past by the standards of the present.'

Margaret Thatcher

Margaret Thatcher wrote this, quoting Lord Acton, in her foreword to an essay written by Professor Hugh Thomas for the Centre of Policy Studies called 'History, Capitalism and Freedom'. It was 1979 and she was on the verge of becoming Britain's first woman prime minister. In her foreword she bemoaned the insidious way that socialist historians denigrated the period of our greatest progress in the eighteenth and nineteenth centuries.

Thirty years later, little seems to have changed with our imperial history overshadowed by the story of slavery and the Industrial Revolution darkened by the conditions of the urban poor. My daughter's school history course has been dominated by both these liberal angles.

The same is true of military history. There is a terrible tendency among liberal commentators to fasten on to politically motivated historical clichés that misunderstand the past. In their eyes, the First World War is now characterized by the first day of the Somme as a pointless war of mud and blood, forgetting the motivations of the men at the time. As Somme veteran Sidney Rogerson wrote in 1933: 'Life in the trenches was not all ghastliness. It was a compound of many things: fright and boredom, humour, comradeship, tragedy, weariness, courage, and despair.'

HELEN J. NICHOLSON

*"'And what is the use of a book," thought Alice,
"without pictures or conversation?"'*

Lewis Carroll, *Alice in Wonderland*

Lewis Carroll (Charles Dodgson) was a mathematician and a philosopher rather than an historian, but the philosophy of the Alice books is applicable to any realm of life. Many a historian follows the White Queen in *Through the Looking Glass*, believing 'as many as six impossible things before breakfast', accepting the latest historical craze even though it flies in the face of all common sense. Most of us know what it is like to run the Red Queen's race, running as fast as we can just 'to keep in the same place'. But Alice's views on books are particularly intriguing, because as a mathematician, much of Carroll's writing had no pictures or conversation – and thus was beyond the interest of most of the population. So what was its use?

I ask the same about much historical writing. Even when they are based on laborious research into the sources and a good understanding of human nature (and many are not) the majority of serious history books are extremely dry. So dry that the *Wonderland* Mouse claimed that a dose of history could dry out a crowd of dripping wet people – Alice, however, found that it couldn't even do that: 'it doesn't seem to dry me at all'. So the crowd resorted to a Caucus-Race, where – Alice fans will recall – everyone can join in, everyone wins and gets a prize.

Serious historians are still very cautious about making history accessible to non-specialists. Serious history books don't have pictures, and those that do are, by definition, not serious history books. So, throughout my three years of research for my history doctorate on medieval images of Templars, Hospitallers and Teutonic Knights, I saw hardly any medieval pictures of these religious warriors. Clearly it's ridiculous to study a group of people for so long without being able to find out what they looked like, and now I collect and publish medieval pictures in my books whenever I can. I believe that historians should use all the sources which survive from the period they are studying: writing, artefacts, buildings, art. Then, perhaps, the history we write will be a truer picture of the past, and much more use to everyone who reads it.

IT FEELS
LIKE SOMEONE
IS HOLDING
MY LEGS
WHEN I WALK

Linda

Every hour, someone in the UK is told they have Parkinson's. Because we're here no one has to face Parkinson's alone.

People like Linda can find everyday activities like walking, eating or getting dressed, difficult or impossible.

People with Parkinson's don't have enough of a chemical called dopamine because some nerve cells in their brain have died.

As the UK's Parkinson's support and research charity, we're leading the work to find a cure, and we're closer than ever.

Our work is totally dependant on donations. Help us find a cure and improve life for everyone affected by Parkinson's.

To donate call 020 7932 1303 or visit parkinsons.org.uk/donate

0808 800 0303
parkinsons.org.uk

DAVID NICOLLE

'Destiny seems to have forgotten me, so that now I am like
An exhausted camel left by the caravan in the desert.'

Usamah Ibn Murshid Ibn Munqidh, *Reminiscences*

As a very young member of the Banu Munqidh Arab clan, Usamah Ibn Murshid was only four years old when the army of the First Crusade swarmed past his ancestral home, the Syrian castle and town of Shayzar. Thereafter Usamah spent most of his life deeply involved in the often chaotic and always tumultuous military and political affairs of Syria, Egypt and what is now south-eastern Turkey. He was a warrior, a middle-ranking military leader, a diplomat and a generally unsuccessful political intriguer. Given his extraordinary life, it is all the more remarkable that he lived long enough to hear of Saladin's crushing of the Crusader Kingdom of Jerusalem at the Battle of Hattin and his liberation of the Holy City of Jerusalem. By then Usamah had long lain his sword aside, and had earned a reputation as a significant – if still occasionally controversial – cultural figure.

For modern historians, of course, it is his *Kitab al-I'tibar* ('Book of Learning by Example'), a collection of recollections or anecdotes, which makes Usamah Ibn Murshid so important. They shed a penetrating light not only on events and personalities, but on the attitudes and motivations, personal foibles, strengths and weaknesses, of a remarkable array of Muslim and other participants in the struggles we now know as 'The Crusades'. Above all, perhaps, they show that the men and women of the twelfth century were essentially the same as those of the twenty-first century. Indeed, the complex and sophisticated society of the twelfth-century Islamic Middle East often seems closer to us than do the frequently fanatical, savage and all too often childlike representatives of Crusader Christendom.

JOHN JULIUS NORWICH

'How these curiosities would be quite forgott, did not such idle fellowes as I put them down.'

John Aubrey, *Brief Lives*

These words by John Aubrey have remained in my mind since I first read them, at least half a century ago. They have justified many a dotty little anecdote that I have been unable to resist including in my history books, and many an entry in the annual anthologies that I call – for want of a better title – my *Christmas Crackers*.

Was Aubrey a historian? Hardly, perhaps; he was barely even a writer, and his editors have had their work cut out even to make a proper volume from the chaotic notebooks and odd scraps of paper that he left behind. The best of them – Oliver Lawson Dick – writes in 1949: 'Any facts or dates that did not occur to him on the spur of the moment were left blank, and as Aubrey was so extremely sociable that he was usually suffering from a hangover when he came to put pen to paper, the number of these omissions was often very large . . . he rarely made a fair copy of anything that he had written because, as he confessed, he "wanted patience to go thorough [*sic*] Knotty Studies".'

And yet, and yet . . . is there any other book that manages to recreate the whole atmosphere, the whole flavour and smell of seventeenth-century England as brilliantly as *Brief Lives*? I know of none. They, surely, are the perfect justification for the grasshopper mind.

MATTHEW PARRIS

'In the socialist state, it is the past that is unpredictable.'

Sir Percy Cradock

Sir Percy's thought, which has certainly been thought before, was ne'er so well expressed as in his valedictory despatch as British ambassador in Peking in December 1983 that comes after the following passage.

'Mao's victims have been rehabilitated, headed by Liu Shaoqui, the former President, and Liu's widow, Wang Guangmei, who I remember paraded in obloquy and derision before Red Guard rallies in 1967, adorned with a necklace of ping pong balls to represent her bourgeois pearls, is now a great lady, anxiously deferred to wherever she appears. So time brings in its revenges.'

A very similar thought was expressed beautifully by Paul Flynn, the Labour MP for Newport West. Mr Flynn was heard to say: 'With New Labour only the future is certain, the past is always changing!'

JONATHAN POWELL

'Whoever wants to foretell the future must consider the past, for human events ever resemble those of preceding times.'

Niccolò Machiavelli, *The Prince*

In politics, as in most areas of human endeavour, it is terribly easy to get obsessed by the crisis of the moment. Harold Wilson correctly observed that 'a week is a long time in politics', and while many repeat his maxim very few actually appear to appreciate what it means in practice. The politicians who succeed are those who do. They have a sense of perspective and can see that whatever the crisis is, it will not last forever and events will move on.

When I was in government it seemed that every week from November 1997 to June 2007 the media were telling us that the preceding week had been Tony Blair's 'worst week ever'. In the face of this barrage, it is all too easy to fall into a bunker mentality and to hunker down rather than appreciate what is happening in the broad sweep of events.

Machiavelli was the first to observe the need for leaders to have this sense of historical perspective. He wrote in *The Discourses* that 'if the present be compared with the remote past, it is easily seen that in all cities and in all people there are the same desires and the same passions as there always were. So that, if one examines with diligence the past, it is easy to foresee the future of any commonwealth, and to apply those remedies which were used of old . . . But, since such studies are neglected and what is read is not understood, or if it be understood, is not applied in practice by those who rule, the consequence is that similar troubles occur all the time.'

His follower, James Harrington, in *Oceana*, written in the seventeenth century, captured the thought even more pithily: 'No man can be a politician, except he first be a Historian or a Traveller, for . . . he that neither knows what has been, nor what is, can never tell what must be, nor what may be.'

The truth of this insight, that politicians need to study the past and gain from it a sense of perspective about events, was brought home to me vividly about two years into government when Tony Blair mused to me in the margins of a meeting in Downing Street, that he wished when he was at university that rather than law he had studied something useful for his job. Something like history.

JONATHAN POWELL

On Wednesday 8 April 1998, Tony Blair and his entourage swept past the media scrum into Hillsborough Castle outside Belfast, the stately home that served as the vice-regal bed and breakfast for the British Secretary of State for Northern Ireland.

On the way over the Irish Sea, we had decided that there was no need for Tony to do a 'doorstep' for the press. After all, he had come over to Belfast against the advice of all the experts, who said there was no chance of an agreement, and essentially without a plan. As we walked into the Castle, however, Alastair Campbell decided that Tony should say something to set the context for the talks and we propelled him straight back out to the waiting cameras in the entrance lobby.

Tony did not have time to prepare as he would usually do for such a statement on TV. Normally he would work on phrases and turn them over and over in his mouth in advance. But we were anxious to get on with the negotiations and didn't give him the chance. As a result he came up with one of his most awkward, but also one of his most memorable, statements as Prime Minister, saying, 'A day like today is not a day for soundbites, we can leave those at home. But I feel the hand of history upon our shoulder with respect to this, I really do.'

Alastair and I, hovering by the door, collapsed in fits of giggles. When we asked Tony afterwards how he had come up with 'the hand of history' he simply couldn't explain it. He said the phrase had just popped into his head.

After three days and nights of negotiation in Castle Buildings it felt as though the hand of history had grabbed another part of our anatomy. Reeling from lack of sleep and the emotional roller-coaster of the negotiations we flopped into an RAF helicopter with a crew member sitting with his legs hanging out of the open door as we took off with a huge machine gun pointing down at the ground below us. There wasn't even time to take the congratulatory call from the Queen as the helicopter became airborne.

Tony's soundbite had been prophetic. History had been made, even if it had been extremely painful in the process and even if it took us a further nine years actually to implement the Good Friday Agreement and bring what I hope is lasting peace to Northern Ireland.

LAURENCE REES

Never give up
No matter what is going on
Never give up

Develop the heart
Too much energy in your country
Is spent on developing the mind
Instead of the heart
Develop the heart

Be compassionate
Not just to your friends
But with everyone
Be compassionate

Work for peace
In your heart
And in the world
Work for peace

And I say again
Never give up
No matter what is going on around you
Never give up.

Tenzin Gyatso, Fourteenth Dalai Lama

My favourite quote comes from the current Dalai Lama. It's the first verse of a prayer/meditation, and is a deceptively simple instruction. It's reminiscent of the words Churchill used in a famous speech at Harrow School in 1941, when he said: 'Never give in. Never give in. Never, never, never, never – in nothing, great or small, large or petty – never give in, except to convictions of honour and good sense.'

But I think there is a great deal of difference between 'never give up' (which, interestingly, is often how Churchill's words are misquoted) and 'never give in'. The latter has a bellicose quality to it – something, of course Churchill wanted to convey – whilst the former is much more of a personal reminder of how best to approach life.

The words 'never give up' also have a particular poignancy to them when one considers they come from the Dalai Lama, a man whose commitment to non-violence has been cruelly tested over the last fifty years or more by the Chinese occupation of Tibet. Indeed it's quite extraordinary, given this background, that he is able to offer the level of compassionate inspiration he does, something he expresses in another of his injunctions: 'Be kind whenever possible. It is always possible.'

JONATHON RILEY

'The Franco-Prussian War was caused by the Queen of Spain's drawers; or more precisely, the rapidity and frequency of their descent.'

Richard Holmes

Richard Holmes had a magical gift for bringing that other country, the past, right into the present. Through his many books, his public lectures and above all his television programmes, he made history accessible to everyone – and he made it fun. In this quotation, he is describing the *casus belli* between Prussia and Germany in 1870, something that might usually cause one to plump up one's pillow: how the debauched Queen Isabella II of Spain went too far, was deposed by a military coup and left the throne vacant. The nearest family in line that was non-Bourbon and Catholic was German and the Spanish Cortes accordingly offered the throne to Prince Leopold of Hohenzollern-Sigmaringen. The prince's relationship with the royal house of Prussia was too much for the French; a confrontation ensued, during which the Ems telegram provided Bismarck with the opportunity he sought for war.

I remember Richard coming out with this classic line during a Higher Command and Staff Course study period at Sedan when he was the course lead historian and I was the director, the evening before a terrain tour. The students, intent on drinks and a good dinner, forgot these things and were at once hooked. He then went on to describe the opening phases of the war up to the Battle of Sedan lucidly, simply and engagingly, as only he could, for he had a way with words and could turn a phrase like no one else. This was more than entertainment, however. Richard used his gift for imparting his encyclopaedic knowledge, cut with penetrating analysis, to help educate generations of military officers. Beginning at Sandhurst, later at the Army Staff College and later still at the Joint Services Command and Staff College, he was one of those who brought the study of military history back from the periphery of military study, to its core. In doing so he helped to guide the intellectual development of many senior commanders who have had to deal with the complexities and dangers of the post-Cold War and post-9/11 world.

But he never fell into the trap of thinking that because he knew more about history than his students did, he therefore knew more than they did about that other great teacher, war. Richard was a distinguished reserve army officer. He was a captain and major in the 5th Queen's and commanded the company based in the old Victorian Drill Hall at Sandford Terrace, Guildford. By sheer force of personality, professionalism and example, he raised this company to be the largest in the whole of the Territorial Army. He transferred to the Wessex Regiment – effectively the TA battalion of the Royal Hampshires – to command them. This made him a natural choice as Colonel of the Regiment later on, after the amalgamation of The Queen's and the Royal Hampshires. He rose to be the senior reserve officer in the Army and it was his legacy that raised the rank of this post from brigadier to major general. But as he himself often remarked, he had never heard a shot fired in anger, while being very aware that many of his students had done so many times. He was always careful, therefore, that the role of lead historian should be to provide historical example, context, the long view – not to tell anyone how to do their job, nor to sit in judgement over those who in the past had been faced with hard decisions in difficult circumstances.

None of us who knew him will ever forget him, nor forget our debt to him. He leaves a gap in our lives and in our country that cannot be filled.

ANDREW ROBERTS

'The past is a quicksand, a lottery, a harlot and a hall of mirrors. That's why we are so fascinated by it.'

TREVOR ROYLE

'We, the most distant dwellers upon earth, the last of the free,
have been shielded till today by our very remoteness and by the
obscurity in which it has shrouded our name. Now, the farthest
bounds of Britain lie open to our enemies; and what men know
nothing about they always assume to be a valuable prize.
But there are no more nations beyond us; nothing is there
but waves and rocks, and the Romans, more deadly still than
these – for in them is an arrogance which no submission or
good behaviour can escape. Pillagers of the world, they have
exhausted the land by their indiscriminate plunder, and now
they ransack the sea. A rich enemy excites their cupidity;
a poor one, their lust for power . . . To robbery, butchery,
and rapine they give the lying name of "government";
they create a desolation and they call it peace.'

Tacitus, *Agricola*

War is such an unnatural event that we struggle to come to terms with its existence and have difficulty finding the necessary rhetoric to describe its many moods and challenges. Usually war is a last resort, the final throw of the dice when all has failed and violence takes the place of reason. Sometimes wars are fought for honourable reasons. The good fight of the Second World War to extirpate the evil of fascism is an obvious example but sometimes wars spring into being for reasons which are immoral or illegal or both.

In 2003 a US-led coalition army invaded Iraq to oust the regime of President Saddam Hussein. There was nothing particularly wrong with the motive – regime change has been employed many times in the past – but in this case the operation was based on flawed evidence and was instigated for reasons which had more to do with imposing US hegemony on a region where Western motives have always been distrusted. When it became clear that the coalition had little idea how to impose order and Iraq fell victim to a vicious insurgency war, I was constantly reminded of the words put into the mouth of the swordsman Calgacus by the Roman historian Tacitus. Before the Battle of Mons Graupius, fought around 84 CE in a location which has never been found, Calgacus roused the soldiers of his Caledonian confederation with sentiments which would be readily understood by anyone facing unwelcome invaders.

PHILIP SABIN

'In the whole range of human activities, war most closely resembles a game of cards.'

Carl von Clausewitz, *On War*

This seemingly bizarre analogy by the great theorist of war in fact captures an important truth – that war is unusual in comparison to the broad range of individual or cooperative human endeavours, and that its inherent conflict compares most to the artificial contests of the world of games.

Whereas in everyday life we are preoccupied with efficiency and trust, in war (as in games) paradoxical approaches such as bluffing and doing the unexpected come to the fore. This analogy has been exploited through analytical techniques such as 'game theory' and 'wargaming', and I use such methods extensively myself when trying to model the dynamics of this most awful but compelling aspect of human history.

DOMINIC SANDBROOK

'History is the great propagator of doubt.'

A. J. P. Taylor

For all his undoubted greatness, A. J. P. Taylor was wrong about a lot of things. This, though, was not one of them. Politicians love to talk about the lessons of history, seeking justification in the past before launching some hideous new venture, but for anyone who seriously thinks about history, the only proper reaction is surely awe at the sheer complexity of events and outcomes. Taylor's immersion in the past explains why he was one of the great British sceptics, for the closer you look at the record of human history, the harder it becomes to make out a clear pattern. And the more history I read, the more I think about the impossibly chaotic and confused lives of all the people who came before me, the harder it becomes to believe in fixed lessons and timeless verities. Historians often write to show off, to make a name for themselves, to impress themselves on their readers and their professions, but one of the great underrated qualities is humility. And though Taylor was hardly a paragon of humility himself, he was dead right: the more you study history, the more you realize what you don't know and the more you question what you thought you did. It's a great lesson for any young historian: don't be afraid to admit that sometimes you just don't know, and never forget that you might be wrong.

CHRISTOPHER SAUNDERS

'South Africa has advanced politically by disasters and economically by windfalls.'

C. W. de Kiewiet, *A History of South Africa, Social and Economic*

Many have quoted this sentence from a classic short history of South Africa by Cornelis de Kiewiet as an appropriate description of South Africa's development. De Kiewiet was a master of the pithy saying, and this line referred particularly to the discovery of diamonds in the late 1860s in the centre of what would become the united country of South Africa in 1910. The discovery of the largest gold deposits ever found in 1886 was an even greater windfall, without which the country would not have developed as it did in the twentieth century. De Kiewiet, who was already in exile when he wrote this line, saw the political development of the country towards increased racial segregation as a disaster. He lived to see South Africa move, under apartheid, towards racial civil war, but he died before the relatively peaceful end of apartheid and the advent of a new democracy in the 1990s. Though some commentators today see the dominance of the ANC and its toleration of corrupt practices as another 'disaster', this aphorism, on close analysis, fails to capture the complexities of the country's history.

GUY SAVILLE

'History is written by the winners.'

George Orwell, 4 February 1944

Orwell's words were true of the history that preceded them, and even more prescient for what was to follow.

In the years since the Second World War, the winners' version of events has been repeated with such conviction that many people now have a distorted view of history. Instead of the complex reality, there is the myth of Britain's 'finest hour' or Russia's 'Great Patriotic War', while the United States has positioned itself as saviour of the free world. In short, the victors turned the war into a Manichean struggle between the forces of good and the evils of Nazism.

This is not to condone or exonerate the crimes of the Third Reich, but the truth is less black and white: as Graham Greene would have it 'more like black and grey'. I believe we must disseminate incidents such as Britain's bombing of Dresden (where 24,000 civilians died in a single air raid) or the Red Army's record of sexual violence as it fought its way to Berlin. Recently, historians have begun to expose this carnage – but an aura of moral sanctimony still cloaks the Allies' account of themselves between 1939 and 1945.

Why is it important to challenge the winners' depiction of history? Not doing so risks complacency and accepting the belief we are always on the right – and righteous – side. It ignores the fact that terrible things can be inflicted on the vanquished. The Manichean view denies us empathy. Subsequent conflicts, such as Vietnam and Iraq, can be seen partly as the legacy of this.

That is why I have always been fascinated by alternative histories: they force us to reconsider our presumptions. A world which saw the Third Reich victorious supposes a history of a very different hue. If we follow Orwell's assertion, it would turn the triumphs of the Allies into war crimes; Nazi atrocities would become acts of heroism necessary to safeguard civilization. If this seems shocking or unpalatable – that's my point. It makes us realize how subjective history is.

Without the dubious certainties we cling to, we are more likely to question not only the past but the present. That can only benefit the future.

DESMOND SEWARD

'I believe that the supreme duty of the historian is to write history, that is to say, to attempt to record in one sweeping sequence the greater events and movements that have swayed the destinies of man.'

Sir Steven Runciman, preface to *A History of the Crusades*

The historian I most admire was Sir Steven Runciman, whom I knew well. Although I am not a Byzantinist as he was, he taught me a lot about his approach to writing history – an unfashionable one, yet he was among his century's most successful historians. The quotation is his protest against modern historians producing what he called 'narrowly specialized dissertations'. He believed that perfection is impossible when painting a broad picture, but you must do your best. (Ironically, this is true of his *History of the Crusades*, overtaken by modern scholarship.)

Not so much a revisionist as seeking the truth, he was critical of today's historians for an emphasis on documentary research that, in his view, often ended in producing 'just another secondary source'. His own approach was epitomized by his first book, *The Emperor Romanus Lecapenus*, on a monarch hitherto considered of no account. Using Armenian and Syriac sources – he read both languages – Runciman showed how this obscure tenth-century ruler had by skilful diplomacy kept the Turks out of Anatolia, and that abandoning his policies ultimately led to the Ottoman conquest of Byzantium.

Some of his rivals dismissed Runciman as a 'narrative historian', which he took as a compliment. (He said of another Crusader historian, 'the man thinks it a sin to write readably'.) Readability was among his great strengths – his *Crusades* are still in print – and in more than a few ways he resembled Gibbon. Asked, however, on whom he modelled his style, he always answered 'Beatrix Potter – think of Mrs Rabbit telling Peter to be careful and remember what happened to his father who ended in a pie. Let the story tell itself!'

GARY SHEFFIELD

'Approximate precedents.'

Andrew Gordon, *The Rules of the Game: Jutland and British Naval Command*

Unusually perhaps for a university professor I am happy to describe myself as an 'applied historian'. For the first twenty-odd years of my academic career I worked for the British military. I started working for the Army in the Department of War Studies, Royal Military Academy Sandhurst. Later

I moved to the Joint Services Command and Staff College where I was privileged to work as one of three historians on the elite Higher Command and Staff Course (HCSC). The British military do not employ military historians because the subject is interesting, but because it is seen as professionally relevant to military officers. One key aspect of this was learning from the past.

This introduces my favourite quotation, which comes from my former HCSC colleague Dr Andrew Gordon: that there are 'approximate precedents' in military history of relevance to the present. The phrase comes from Andrew's magisterial *The Rules of the Game: Jutland and British Naval Command*, and he assures me that it is an original Gordonism. It sums up so well how military history, if used with care, can provide guidance for modern times, and it was our underlying philosophy for teaching future high commanders on the HCSC. For war is a unique phenomenon, and arguably individual wars and battles that occurred in very different time periods have more in common with each other than with other contemporary but non-military events. Technology has changed radically since the time of Alexander the Great, but the nature of war has not. Neither have some of the fundamentals of warfare. Logistics, challenges of command, the importance of morale, and the elements of strategy are a few facets of war that have remained fairly constant, even after cultural factors and other variables are factored in.

However, to talk of 'learning lessons' from military history is too crude. It is dangerous in the extreme to pillage military history for examples that support a particular battle plan or doctrine, although too often military officers have used this 'cherry-picking' approach. It is the job of the applied historian gently but firmly to point out that this is wrong. As Sir Michael Howard argued nearly fifty years ago, military history should be studied in breadth, as well as in depth, and should be placed into context. Using the concept of 'approximate precedents' emphasizes the value of military history while discouraging the idea that the past provides a template for the present. Officers planning Operation Desert Storm, the offensive to retake Kuwait from the Iraqis in 1991, drew upon the Battle of Cannae in 216 BCE and modern Soviet operational doctrine that stemmed from the Second World War. Both provided approximate precedents for the task facing the Coalition forces, and were blended into the successful operational design for a late twentieth-century battle.

DENNIS SHOWALTER

'It is well this is so terrible! Otherwise we should grow too fond of it.'

Robert E. Lee, 13 December 1862

Lee, a great soldier and a great gentleman, cuts to the heart of Western civilization's most fundamental ambivalence – its understanding of war. Since the Greeks and before, no societies, no peoples, have sustained their existence without being good at war. Few have fallen without seeking to reverse their decline by force of arms. Nor do clear lines divide most people from most soldiers. War exercises a powerful fascination. Fighting can be a source of honour, of identity, of pleasure. At the same time war by its nature tends toward entropic violence, with neither structure, purpose, nor meaning. Athena, goddess of victory and wisdom, and Janus, with his faces fixed in opposite directions, combine eternally to shape a perspective central to the identity of the 'restless West'.

DAN SNOW

*'In order for things to stay the same, everything will
have to change.'*

Giuseppe Tomasi di Lampedusa, *The Leopard*

This is the single most important 'lesson from history'. Stasis is impossible in human affairs. We are an evolving species living on a hugely dynamic planet. Periods of unchanging continuity are short and in any case are almost certainly illusory. Societies are as vulnerable as individuals to disease and accident, which can destabilize and destroy in an instant.

Today Lampedusa's maxim could not be more relevant. Never has a culture been so comfortable, so certain of its immortality as our own at the beginning of the twenty-first century. Yet the experiment in Western liberal democracy will end as certainly as Rome; one day our Rhine will freeze. The mightiest empires and most sophisticated civilizations are nothing more, as Shakespeare realized, than 'insubstantial pageants'.

As a devoted generalist I have noticed that every period I arrive at is described almost immediately as 'transitional', a conceit which presumes that stability lies just over the horizon in someone else's field. It does not. Human history is anarchic; change is the only constant.

TIMOTHY SNYDER

'What is meant by historical sense is the knowledge not of what happened, but of what did not happen.'

Isaiah Berlin

Every historian, like every human being, begins from the muddle of today, the impossibility of understanding what is happening as it actually happens. The luxury historians have consists in the time and the tools to consider, slowly and critically, a given moment in the past. Over description and interpretation we will, and should, argue, but what we can do is rule out the worst and move towards the best, and develop a kind of reflex about what might and might not have been. In some of us, I like to hope, Berlin's 'historical sense', or 'sense of reality', develops into an ability to discard some of the more unreasonable interpretations of events of our own time, a faculty that might be of use in an age starved of plausibility.

HEW STRACHAN

'When people talk, as they often do, about harmful political influence on the management of war, they are not really saying what they mean. Their quarrel should be with the policy itself, not with its influence. If the policy is right – that is, successful – any intentional effect it has on the conduct of war can only be to the good. If it has the opposite effect the policy itself is wrong.'

Carl von Clausewitz, *On War*

When commentators want to discuss the relationship between war and policy, they too readily quote Clausewitz's aphorism that war is the continuation of policy by other means, without considering the caveats and qualifications to this proposition entered by Clausewitz himself. This quotation is the most remarkable, but not the only example, of how Clausewitz is read selectively. It occurs in the very same chapter as that which advances the core proposition concerning the relationship between war and policy, and it reminds us that policy cannot ask of war that which is contrary to war's own nature. A plan for war, as Clausewitz points out in the conclusion to Chapter 3 of Book VIII of *On War*, needs to be governed 'by the general conclusions to be drawn from the nature of war itself'. It is not even clear whether Clausewitz was convinced that policy was part of war's nature; at times he argued that it stood outside war, an alien element acting in opposition to war's own dynamic. This is not a proposition for which political leaders show much awareness, particularly in democratic states. They need to, if they propose to use war as an instrument of policy.

JULIAN THOMPSON

'Most battles are more like a schoolyard in a rough neighbourhood at recess time than a clash between football giants in the Rose Bowl. They are messy, inorganic, and uncoordinated. It is only much later after the clerks have tidied up their reports and the generals have published their memoirs, that the historian with his orderly mind professes to discern an understandable pattern in what was essentially catch-as-catch-can, if not chaotic, at the time.'

Brigadier General S. L. A. Marshall

This is one of the best descriptions of battle I have read. It is essentially a chaotic activity, and the winners are often those who manage to sort out the chaos the quickest. An experienced commander, especially one who has read history, understands this, and prepares his troops accordingly. The British Brigadier James Hill on the eve of the Normandy operation in June 1944 addressed his 3rd Parachute Brigade thus: 'Gentlemen, in spite of your excellent training and orders, do not be dismayed if chaos reigns; it undoubtedly will.' The American Brigadier General Norman Cota in his address to the 29th US Infantry Division, before they landed on Omaha Beach in Normandy, included the words: 'You're going to find confusion. The landing craft aren't going to go in on schedule, and people are going to be landed in the wrong place. Some won't be landed at all.'

How right they both were.

CLAIRE TOMALIN

E. P. Thompson said he wrote his most famous book to rescue the working class from the condescension of history. I have always admired the formulation, and I set out to write a few books in a similar spirit, to rescue women from the condescension of history.

JOANNA TROLLOPE

'[The Victorians] were lame giants; the strongest of them walked with one leg shorter than the other . . . There is a moment when Carlyle turns suddenly from a high creative mystic to a common Calvinist. There are moments when George Eliot turns from a prophetess into a governess. And there are also moments when Ruskin turns into a governess too, without even the excuse of sex . . .'

G. K. Chesterton

I found this Chesterton quote when researching one of my long-ago historical novels, and found it very appealing, not least because it's slightly disrespectful. I just think that this is funny. It's extra funny because the Victorians were so certain of themselves, and their values, and their world view. Chesterton is simply adding comedy red noses to a row of sacred cows, and the result is cheering, especially for an age like ours when we are infinitely less convinced about anything.

STEPHEN TURNBULL

*'Classes struggle, some classes triumph, others
are eliminated. Such is history.'*

Mao Zedong

The thing I like about Chinese history is that there is so much of it.

I recall being told a story concerning the transfer of one Chinese dynasty
for another. I don't remember which ones they were. Let's say it was the
replacement of the Ming by the Qing. The point of the story is that it

doesn't matter anyway, but we are told that one of the first things the new rulers did was to order the removal of the capstone over the gate at Beijing that bore the enormous carved character that said 'Ming'. The workmen chiselled it out after considerable effort and were about to smash it to pieces when a Qing official intervened. It was actually a rather beautiful object, and after all the Ming had been around for three centuries, so it was decided to keep it. It was too heavy to lower to the ground, so the official suggested they stick it into a little room up there on the parapet that their stonework had just exposed. They forced the door open, and lying inside they found capstones saying 'Yuan', 'Song', 'Tang', 'Sui' . . . well, it's only a story.

CHRISTOPHER TYERMAN

'History is all things to all men. She is at the service of good causes and bad. In other words she is a harlot and a hireling and for this reason she best serves those who suspect her most.'

Herbert Butterfield

A common misunderstanding is that history is a synonym for the past and that historians study that past. They do not and cannot. Historians study the remains of the past that exist in the present. Therefore any view of that past is partial, incomplete, contingent, its interpretation necessarily inviting the tendentious and partisan. Butterfield reminds us that, just as or perhaps because history lacks any claim to absolute or objective truth, it lends itself to manipulation and distortion. History is neutral; it is the sum of surviving evidence. Of itself it lacks any moral or didactic dimension until given such by historians. Thus it can be used to support anachronistic political, ideological or cultural interests, right or left, religious or secular, nationalist or imperial. This is as true of promoters of US providential exceptionalism or the superiority of Western capitalism as it was for Stalin, Franco or Goebbels.

Nowhere is this more obvious than in my own area of particular study, the Crusades. Memories of the medieval wars of religion remain toxic, a living popular grievance from the Near East to Greece to the eastern Baltic. Yet what is traded is not fact but sentiment framed by contemporary cultural assumptions, moulded to suit authors and the audiences. Protestants regarded the Crusades as religiously corrupt. Enlightenment savants disdained their fanaticism. Nineteenth-century Romantics and nationalists branded them as signs of positive cultural energy, religious spirit and proto-colonialism, part of a supposed ageless struggle between some constructed idea of 'West' and 'East'. Recently such materialist views have been joined by appreciation of the Crusades as ideological warfare made newly familiar over the last century.

The only fixed certainty comes not from historical understanding but polemical visions of a convenient invented past, an especial danger for generalists and those seeking to lump history into neat patterns. By challenging competing interpretations and popular, not uncommonly malign historical myths, the critical study of history liberates; its misuse can enslave minds, bodies and whole societies.

TED VALLANCE

'No man can have in his mind a conception of the future, for the future is not yet. But of our conceptions of the past, we make a future.'

Thomas Hobbes, *The Elements of Law*

This quotation from the seventeenth-century political philosopher Thomas Hobbes seems deceptively straightforward: the past provides us with a storehouse of precedents which we can use to reasonably predict how things will pan out in the future. But, of course, Hobbes was too subtle a thinker to be lured into asserting that the lessons of history provided a sure guide to future actions – experience, he said, 'concludeth nothing universally'.

To me, the beauty of this quotation is the way it encapsulates both the centrality of history to human existence and the complexity of our relationship with the past. Our actions are guided by what we think has gone before, but our perception of history is inevitably present-centred and subjective.

Read broadly, deeply and sensitively, history can profoundly enrich our understanding of the present and, indeed, help us make informed judgements about the future. Read selectively, through partisan eyes, history can be a powerful, destructive force. Hobbes himself saw historical knowledge as directly leading his country to catastrophe. In his *Behemoth*, published in 1668, he fixed upon the teaching of classical history in universities as a root cause of the English Civil War. In these histories, Hobbes said, 'the popular government was extolled by that glorious name of liberty, and monarchy disgraced by the name of tyranny; they became thereby in love with their forms of government'. Given history's power, no wonder successive twentieth- and twenty-first-century education secretaries have been so eager to dictate the terms of the school curriculum!

CHARLES VAN ONSELEN

'Unless we ourselves take a hand now, they will foist a
republic on us. If we want things to stay as they are,
things will have to change.'

Giuseppe Tomasi di Lampedusa, *The Leopard*

Historians – and more especially social historians – have much to learn
from the best writers of fiction. Good novelists have mastered the art of
maintaining a lively narrative pace without abandoning the simultaneous
need to do justice to process and structure, one of the core skills when it
comes to the art of history writing. Great novelists also have the enviable
ability of gliding effortlessly over terrain historians recognize as tough
going – contradiction, irony and paradox. The insights of our craft cousins
can be pertinent, sometimes salutary.

Giuseppe di Lampedusa's *The Leopard* offers one of the finest two-
sentence tutorials any young historian could ever ask for. The Prince,
sensing the mounting threat to the monarchy, warns his nephew to exercise
caution when making his choice of both cause and company. Tancredi
offers the subtle reply above.

There are profound lessons in this for anyone wishing to understand the
agonizingly slow death of twentieth-century apartheid South Africa, or the
longevity of so many other authoritarian states in Africa. In South Africa
a white minority made increasingly fruitless attempts to effect changes in
the hope of keeping things the same. The ability to detect the point where
continuity gives way to real change is central to any persuasive historical
analysis. Sensing where that difference lies is one of the key challenges
confronting South Africa's new elite.

GERHARD L. WEINBERG

*'History teaches us that men and nations behave wisely
once they have exhausted all other alternatives.'*

Abba Ebban

This 1970 quote from the Israeli diplomat and politician Abba Ebban is surely a helpful way for both historians and the general public to approach the history of Germany in modern times. Some of the alternatives exhausted by first Prussia and then Germany may look most puzzling if not regarded this way. It was soon after a Russian army had been in Berlin during the Seven Years War that Frederick II, often called 'The Great', joined Russia and Austria in the first partition of Poland. He invented the idea of an east–west corridor separating Poland from its port at Danzig (taken by Prussia), while simultaneously bringing Russia further toward central Europe. The allegedly 'Great' idea of bringing Russia ever closer to Prussia-Germany would be pursued by successive Prussian and German governments until the Russian army again entered Berlin in 1945. It took the government of Helmut Kohl to see the value in what might have been obvious earlier: an independent and strong Poland as a form of protection for Germany's eastern border, however drawn, requiring a push for the admission of Poland to NATO. Numerous other examples could be cited such as the rapprochement of Germany with France in foreign affairs and the wide acceptance of a parliamentary democracy in internal affairs. Some of the alternatives Germany exhausted, such as the extensive murders in the so-called euthanasia programme and the Holocaust, would not have been expected by observers of the country a hundred years ago, but these have been followed by vastly different and more humane approaches to difficult challenges that Germany, like all countries, has had to face from time to time. Perhaps the Israeli diplomat had it right.

KEITH WINDSCHUTTLE

'The theologian may indulge the pleasing task of describing Religion as she descended from Heaven, arrayed in her native purity. A more melancholy duty is imposed on the historian. He must discover the inevitable mixture of error and corruption, which she contracted in a long residence upon earth, among a weak and degenerate race of beings.'

Edward Gibbon, *The History of the Decline and Fall of the Roman Empire*

'And class happens when some men, as a result of common experiences (inherited or shared), feel and articulate the identity of their interests as between themselves, and as against other men whose interests are different from (and usually opposed to) theirs.'

E. P. Thompson, *The Making of the English Working Class*

To my mind, Gibbon's is the best advice any historian has ever given to his fellows. It applies not only to the history of religion but to all fields of the discipline, especially political history. Don't sentimentalize or glorify any cause, let alone try to convince people they can make heaven on earth. The quest is forever futile; the outcome doomed to be tragic.

In my generation, the worst offender against Gibbon's advice was the historian I spent more than a decade of my youth vainly trying to emulate: Edward Thompson, the Communist Party dissident who in 1963 wrote *The Making of the English Working Class*. Thompson was the historian I once admired most. His research seemed meticulous and exhaustive, his prose passionate and combative, his empathy with the wretched of the earth compelling. Almost single-handedly, Thompson created 'history from below', or social history, a movement his followers subsequently entrenched within the universities, thereby converting much of the discipline from scholarly pursuit to ideological dogma. In the long run, his concept of the class struggle was revealed as a sociological fiction – an abstract theory imposed on the evidence and, worse, on the very people Thompson championed. Wherever the Communist Party gained power,

the class struggle, and the insidious moral relativism embedded within it, sanctioned political murder on a mass scale.

As Gibbon observed in 1776, theology is a pleasing task but the story of its residence on Earth is another matter. By the time Edward Thompson died in 1993, the Communist creed his history was written to serve had collapsed, with nothing to show for it but a death toll of 100 million people.

GORDON S. WOOD

'History is philosophy teaching by example.'
Dionysius of Halicarnassus

This ancient saying is generally attributed to Dionysius of Halicarnassus, Greek historian of the first century BCE, who cited Thucydides as his source. In the eighteenth century Lord Bolingbroke made the aphorism famous for the English-speaking world. Eighteenth-century political leaders read Plutarch's *Lives* with the hope of learning how to govern.

Today such a view of history may still command the allegiance of many people, especially those looking for incidents of heroism or altruism to emulate. But probably most historians would not put much stock in this idea that history is philosophy teaching by example. Following the cataclysmic events of the French Revolution and the writings of Hegel and others, many nineteenth-century historians (but not Thomas Carlyle) came to believe that the past could no longer be understood as a series of discrete actions by heroic individuals. Instead, they came to see the collective actions of millions of people creating a complex historical process that overwhelms the deeds of distinct individuals. Most historians today tend to see events in the past as so unusual, if not unique, as so complicated, and as so much a part of a particular and different time and place that such events are scarcely capable of teaching us any specific lessons.

In so far as history teaches any lessons, it seems to teach only one big one: that nothing ever works out quite the way the participants in the past intended or expected. By showing that the best-laid plans of people in the past usually went awry, the study of history reveals the degree to which past generations were captivated by illusions; indeed, the historical process is really a record of each generation's exploded illusions. But lest we become arrogant and condescending toward the past, we should acknowledge that we too live with illusions, only we don't know what they are. Ultimately, the only lesson history teaches is humility.

EPHRAIM ZUROFF

'Jews, take revenge.'

Anon., Kovno, 1941

'Jews, write down everything.'

Shimon Dubnov, Riga, 1941

Two 'quotes' related to the history of the Holocaust have remained etched in my consciousness for many years. The first was inscribed in the summer of 1941 on a wall of a Jewish apartment in the Slobodka suburb of the city of Kovno (Kaunas), Lithuania, following a wave of murderous attacks by the Nazis' Lithuanian collaborators. '*Yidn nekoma*' ('Jews, take revenge') was the final will and testament scrawled as a plea in response to the brutal murders carried out by Lithuanian vigilantes and police against their Jewish neighbours in the aftermath of the Nazi invasion of 22 June 1941.

The second quote was recorded several months later, 140 miles away in the city of Riga, Latvia. As he was being dragged out of his home to be murdered by the Nazis and their Latvian collaborators in the winter of 1941–2, the noted Jewish historian Shimon Dubnov told the Jews around him '*Yidn farschreibt*' ('Jews, write down everything').

These ostensibly contradictory quotes, one by an anonymous Jew calling for revenge, the other by a famous Jewish historian urging a recording of all the crimes, have had a unique resonance for me over the past thirty years as I attempted to find, expose, and facilitate the prosecution of Holocaust perpetrators all over the world. As a young academic specializing in the history of the Holocaust I had initially begun by following Dubnov's exhortation but, as fate would have it, my studies ultimately led me to search for the perpetrators, a pursuit closer to the request/demand of the anonymous Jew from Kovno. In that regard I believe that I was influenced by my activist youth as a campaigner for Soviet Jewry and Israel's security, causes which inevitably were inspired by the failures of my parents' generation to prevent the Holocaust or significantly to limit the Nazis' murderous crimes.

In retrospect, I feel that I have ultimately tried to fulfil the wishes of both Dubnov and the anonymous Jew from Kovno. There are many ways to take revenge, and this does not necessarily mean carrying out extrajudicial executions. By helping to bring Nazi war criminals to justice, we are facilitating their punishment but also indelibly inscribing their crimes and guilt in the historical record, thereby achieving a type of *nekoma*, while ensuring that the atrocities will be recorded for posterity.

Index of Contributors

The majority of the biographies that follow have been supplied by the contributors but in a few cases the editor has written missing entries.

Charles Allen British writer and historian. His many books on India include *Plain Tales from the Raj* and *Kipling Sahib*.

Joyce Appleby Emerita Professor at UCLA who studies the intellectual response to changes in the material world.

Rick Atkinson Author of *An Army at Dawn* and *The Day of Battle*.

Juliet Barker Biographer and historian; her works include *The Brontes* and *Agincourt*.

Correlli Barnett Appointed CBE in 1997, a military historian and Fellow of Churchill College, Cambridge.

Mary Beard Professor of Classics at Cambridge.

Antony Beevor Author of *Stalingrad, Berlin, The Battle for Spain* and *D-Day: The Battle for Normandy*.

Martin Bell Former BBC war reporter.

Alan Bennett English playwright and actor.

Conrad Black Canadian-born historian and publisher.

Jeremy Black Historian and Professor of History.

Geoffrey Blainey Professor of History at the University of Exeter.

Michael Bliss Author and historian and Emeritus Professor at the University of Toronto.

Richard Bosworth Winthrop Professor of History, UWA, and Professor of History at Reading University. His next work, *Whispering City: Rome and its Histories*, will be published in 2011.

Asa Briggs Historian and former Chancellor of the Open University and Provost of Worcester College, Oxford.

Ken Burns Author and film-maker, winner of ten Emmy Awards and recipient of two Oscar nominations. His film work includes *The Civil War* and *Brooklyn Bridge*.

K. N. Chaudhuri Emeritus Vasco da Gama Professor of History at the European University, Florence.

Richard Cohen Visiting Professor of Creative Writing at Kingston University and the author, most recently, of *Chasing the Sun*. He is currently at work on *The History of Historians*.

John Robert Colombo Canadian poet, author and historian.

Peter Corris Australian author with more than seventy published books – novels, histories and biographies – to his credit.

Saul David Professor of War Studies at the University of Buckingham and the author of *The Indian Mutiny*, *Zulu* and *Victoria's Wars*.

William C. Davis Professor of History at Virginia Polytechnic Institute and State University.

Terry Deary Author of the *Horrible History* and *Tudor Terror* series.

Carlo D'Este Retired U.S. Army lieutenant colonel, now a military historian and biographer.

Taylor Downing Award-winning producer of television historical films and an author of several books including *Churchill's War Lab*.

Jonathan Eig Author of *Get Capone: The Secret Plot that Captured America's Most Wanted Gangster*. He is also the author of biographies of Lou Gehrig and Jackie Robinson.

John Elliott Regius Professor Emeritus of Modern History in the University of Oxford.

Richard van Emden Military historian and author.

John English Author of a two-volume biography of Pierre Trudeau. Currently general editor of the *Dictionary of Canadian Biography* and Distinguished Senior Fellow at the Munk School of Global Affairs.

Charles Esdaile School of History, University of Liverpool.

Richard J. Evans Regius Professor of Modern History at the University of Cambridge and author of *The Third Reich At War, 1939–1945*.

Amanda Foreman Historian and biographer; her books include *Georgiana, Duchess of Devonshire* and *A World on Fire*.

Martin Gilbert British historian and biographer of Winston Churchill.

Hermann Giliomee South African historian and author, currently Extraordinary Professor of History at Stellenbosch University.

Donald E. Graves A Canadian military historian who has spent entirely too much of his life in the archives created by Arthur Doughty.

Charlotte Gray Canadian historian; her works include *The Museum Called Canada* and *Reluctant Genius: The Passionate Life and Inventive Mind of Alexander Graham Bell*.

Tom Griffiths W. K. Hancock Professor of History at the Australian National University and author of *Slicing the Silence.*

Chris Hale Author of *Himmler's Crusade,* which won the Gambrinus Giuseppe Mazzotti Prize in 2006, and *Hitler's Foreign Executioners.*

Philip Haythornthwaite Historian and author of over forty books, many on aspects of the Napoleonic Wars.

John Hemming Historian of the conquest of the Incas and Brazil, and of the Amazon and its indigenous peoples.

Eric Hobsbawm British historian and activist.

James Holland Historian of the Second World War.

Richard Holmes 1946–2011, military historian and author. His works include *Redcoat, Tommy* and *Sahib.*

Harold Holzer Author, co-author or editor of some forty books on Lincoln and the Civil War, served for nine years as co-chairman of the Abraham Lincoln Bicentennial Commission. In 2008 he was awarded the National Humanities Medal.

Michael Howard Founder of the Department of War Studies at King's College, London, and subsequently held history chairs at Oxford and Yale Universities. His many works on the history of war and peace include a translation of Clausewitz's *On War.*

Daniel W. Howe Author of *What Hath God Wrought: The Transformation of America, 1815–1848.*

John Hughes-Wilson Author and commentator on military history.

Walter Isaacson Author of biographies of Henry Kissinger, Benjamin Franklin and Steve Jobs.

Nigel Jones Historian, journalist and biographer. His *Countdown to Valkyrie: The Plots to Assassinate Hitler* was published in 2009.

Terry Jones Welsh comedian, screen writer, director and historian.

Anthony Julius Australian author with more than seventy published books – novels, histories and biographies.

Grace Karskens Teacher of Australian history at the University of New South Wales and a leading historian of colonial Australia. Her latest book *The Colony: A History of Early Sydney* won the 2010 Prime Minister's Literary Award for non-fiction.

Ian Kershaw Historian and biographer of Adolf Hitler. Former Professor of History at the University of Sheffield.

Robert J. Kershaw Soldier-author who has contributed to documentary film and the media and written seven books.

Jim Al-Khalili Scientist, author and broadcaster. He is a Professor of Theoretical Physics at the University of Surrey.

Henry Kissinger American politician.

Ian Knight Zulu War historian and author. His books include *Brave Men's Blood* and *The Anatomy of the Zulu Army*

Phillip Knightley Author of ten books of general history, including *Australia: A Biography of the Nation.*

Guido Knopp German journalist and historian.

Andrew Lambert Professor of Naval History, King's College, London.

Paul Lay Editor of *History Today* magazine.

Quentin Letts Political sketchwriter and theatre critic of the *Daily Mail*, and author of *Fifty People Who Buggered Up Britain.*

Leanda de Lisle Historian and commentator.

John Lukacs Hungarian-born American historian, author of more than thirty books.

Robert Lyman New Zealand-born military history author and former British Army officer.

Gavin McLean Historian working for the Ministry for Culture and Heritage in Wellington, New Zealand.

Frank McLynn Biographer and historian who has written more than thirty books.

Hugh McManners Military historian and author who spent eighteen years in the British Army.

Allan Mallinson Author of the Matthew Hervey novels, and *The Making of the British Army.*

John Man British historian and travel author. His works include *Attila: The Barbarian King Who Challenged Rome* and *Kublai Khan.*

Hilary Mantel Author of historical and contemporary fiction. *Wolf Hall*, a novel about Thomas Cromwell, won the 2009 Man Booker Prize.

Justin Marozzi Travel writer and historian, author of *The Man Who Invented History: Travels with Herodotus.*

Michael R. Marrus Chancellor Rose and Ray Wolfe Professor Emeritus of Holocaust Studies and an Adjunct Professor of Law at the University of Toronto and a Fellow of Massey College.

Charles Messenger Former Royal Tank Regiment officer turned military historian, with some forty published books to his name.

Alexander Mikaberidze Assistant Professor of European History at Louisiana State University (Shreveport).

Dan Mills Career soldier and author of *Sniper One*, a book describing his experiences during the war in Iraq.

Christopher Moore A writer in Toronto and the author of, among other works, *Louisbourg Portraits: Life in an Eighteenth Century Garrison Town.*

Roger Moorhouse Historian specialising in the Third Reich. He is the author of *Killing Hitler* and *Berlin at War.*

Melissa Müller Author of the best-selling *Anne Frank: The Biography* and the co-author with Traudl Junge of *Until the Final Hour: Hitler's Last Secretary.*

Bill Nasson University of Stellenbosch.

Tim Newark Former editor of *Military Illustrated*, the leading military history monthly magazine, and numerous military history volumes, including the critically acclaimed *Highlander* and *The Mafia At War.*

Helen J. Nicholson Professional historian and writer. She has been running the Red Queen's Race at Cardiff University since 1994.

David Nicolle English military history author. His works include *Fighting for the Faith: Crusade and Jihad 1000–1500 AD.*

John Julius Norwich Writer, lecturer and historian of Norman Sicily, Venice, Byzantium and the Mediterranean.

Matthew Parris Columnist and author. His books include *Great Parliamentary Scandals*, *Scorn*, *A Castle in Spain* and *Chance Witness.*

Jonathan Powell Formerly Tony Blair's Chief of Staff, now CEO of Inter Mediate an NGO working on conflict resolution.

Laurence Rees British historian and documentary film-maker.

Jonathon Riley Lieutenant General Riley is Director-General and Master of the Royal Armouries and is a writer and historian.

Andrew Roberts English historian and journalist. His works include *The Storm of War: A New History of the Second World War.*

Trevor Royle Broadcaster and author and a Fellow of the Royal Society of Edinburgh.

Philip Sabin Professor of Strategic Studies, King's College London.

Dominic Sandbrook Historian, critic and commentator, best known for his books on modern Britain, most recently *State of Emergency* (2010).

Christopher Saunders Emeritus Professor, Department of Historical Studies, University of Cape Town, South Africa.

Guy Saville Author of *The Afrika Reich*.

Desmond Seward Author of many books, including *The Monks of War: The Military Religious Orders, The Hundred Years War, The Wars of the Roses* and *The Last White Rose*.

Gary Sheffield Professor of War Studies at the University of Birmingham.

Dennis Showalter Professor of History at Colorado College and Past President of the Society for Military History.

Dan Snow Historian and television presenter.

Timothy Snyder Professor of History at Yale, author most recently of *Bloodlands*, a history of Nazi and Stalinist mass killing in eastern Europe.

Hew Strachan Chichele Professor of the History of War and Fellow of All Souls College, Oxford.

Julian Thompson Retired Royal Marines Major General and Visiting Professor in the Department of War Studies, King's College, London.

Claire Tomalin English biographer and journalist, her works include *Samuel Pepys: The Unequalled Self*.

Joanna Trollope British author, writing historical novels as Caroline Harvey.

Stephen Turnbull Until recently Visiting Professor of Japanese Studies at Akita International University in Japan. He specialises in the military history of Japan.

Christopher Tyerman Fellow of Hertford College, Oxford, and author of numerous books on the Crusades, most recently *God's War* (2006).

Ted Vallance Reader in Early Modern British History at Roehampton University and the author of *A Radical History of Britain: Visionaries, Rebels and Revolutionaries, the Men and Women Who Fought for our Freedoms*.

Charles Van Onselen Social historian at the University of Pretoria.

Gerhard L. Weinberg German-born American historian.

Keith Windschuttle Author of *The Killing of History: How a Discipline is Being Murdered by Social Theorists and Literary Critics* and *The Fabrication of Aboriginal History, Volume One* and *Volume Three*.

Gordon S. Wood Alva O. Way University Professor Emeritus at Brown University.

Ephraim Zuroff Holocaust historian and chief Nazi-hunter of the Simon Wiesenthal Center and director of its Israel Office.

Index of Subjects

Arthur G. Doughty 1860–1936, British-born Canadian Dominion archivist.

Shimon Dubnov 1860–1941, historian and writer, victim of the Holocaust.

Lord Durham 1792–1840, British Whig politician.

Abba Ebban 1915–2002, South-African born Israeli diplomat.

Prince Eugene 1663–1736, soldier and statesman of the House of Savoy.

William Faulkner 1897–1962, American writer, Nobel Prize in Literature 1949.

John Arbuthnot Fisher 1841–1920, British admiral.

Ann Frank 1929–45, diarist and victim of the Holocaust.

Clifford Geertz 1926–2006, American cultural anthropologist.

Genghis Khan 1162–1227, Mongolian warrior-ruler.

Edward Gibbon 1737–94, British historian.

Giovanni Giolitti 1842–1928, Italian statesman, five times Prime Minister of Italy.

Andrew Gordon 1951– , British historian.

L. P. Hartley 1895–1972, British writer.

G. W. F. Hegel 1770–1831, German philosopher.

Herodotus *c.* 485–*c.* 425 BCE, Greek historian.

Adolf Hitler 1889–1945, German military and political leader, 1933–45.

Thomas Hobbes 1588–1679, English political philosopher.

Richard Holmes 1946–2011, military historian and author.

Elizabeth Hughes 1907–81, one of the first diabetics to be treated with insulin.

Alexander von Humboldt 1769–1859, German naturalist and explorer.

Al-Hasan Ibn al-Haytham 965–1039, Arab scientist.

Usamah Ibn Murshid Ibn Munqidh *c.* 1090–1190, Syrian military leader, diplomat, politician and writer.

Rhys Isaac 1937–2010, Australian historian.

Tony Judt 1948–2010, British-American historian.

C. W. de Kiewiet 1902–86, Dutch-born American historian.

Henry Kissinger 1923– , American diplomat.

Giuseppe Tomasi di Lampedusa 1896–1957, Italian novelist.

Robert E. Lee 1807–70, American Confederate general.

Emmanuel Le Roy Ladurie 1929– , French historian.

Jean de Lery 1536–1613, French explorer and writer.

Saul Lieberman 1898–1983, Belorussian Rabbi and scholar of the Talmud.

Abraham Lincoln 1809–65, American Republican statesman, sixteenth President of the USA, 1861–65.

David Lowenthal 1923– , American geographer and historian.

Niccolò Machiavelli 1469–1527, Florentine statesman and political philosopher.

Mao Zedong 1893–1976, Chinese communist leader and founder of the People's Republic of China.

S. L. A. Marshall 1900–77, American Army combat historian.

Karl Marx 1818–83, German political philosopher; founder of modern Communism.

Shirley Millard dates unknown, American nurse on the Western Front in the First World War.

George Orwell 1903–50, British writer.

Antonio Pérez 1540–1611, Spanish courtier to King Philip II of Spain.

James Prinsep 1799–1840, British antiquarian and colonial administrator in India.

Tony Robinson 1946– , British actor, broadcaster and political campaigner.

A. L. Rowse 1903–97, British historian.

Steven Runciman 1903–2000, British historian best known for his *A History of the Crusades*.

George Santayana 1863–1952, Spanish writer.

Arthur M. Schlesinger Jr. 1917–2007, American historian.

Ronald Searle 1920– , Artist and cartoonist renowned for creating the St Trinian's School and Molesworth series.

William Slim 1891–1970, British soldier, commander of Fourteenth Army in India and Burma in the Second World War.

Aleksandr Solzhenitsyn 1918–2008, Russian novelist, Nobel Prize in Literature 1970.

Thomas Sowell 1930– , American economist.

Edward Spears 1886–1974, British soldier and politician and key mediator in Anglo-French relations during the First and Second World Wars.

Publius Cornelius Tacitus *c.* 56 CE–after 117, Roman senator and historian.

A. J. P. Taylor 1906–90, British historian.

Margaret Thatcher 1925– , British Conservative stateswoman, Prime Minister 1979–90.

E. P. Thompson 1924–93, British social historian and political activist.

Thucydides *c.* 460–*c.* 395 BCE, Greek historian and author.

G. M. Trevelyan 1876–1962, British historian.

Pierre Trudeau 1919–2000, Canadian Liberal statesman, Prime Minister 1968–79 and 1980–84.

Mark Twain 1835–1910, American writer.

Earl of Uxbridge 1768–1854, British soldier, later Marquess of Anglesey.

Charles Van Onselen 1944– , South African historian.

Gore Vidal 1925– , American novelist and critic.

Voltaire 1694–1778, French writer and philosopher.

Duke of Wellington 1769–1852, British general and statesman, Prime Minister 1828–30, 1834.

Robert Walpole 1676–1745, English Whig statesman; British Prime Minister, 1721–42.

Geoffrey Willans 1911–58, British schoolmaster and author.

'History, like tragedy, requires an exposition, a central action, and a dénouement. My secret is to force the reader to wonder: Will Philip V ascend the throne?'
Voltaire

'It would not be right to have beautiful legends discredited by historical criticism.'
Giovanni Giolitti

'Until lions have their historians, tales of the hunt shall always glorify the hunter.'
Nigerian proverb

Don't read History to me, for I know that can't be true.'
Sir Robert Walpole, 1st Earl of Orford

'As a professor, I tended to think of history as run by impersonal forces. But when you see it in practice, you see the difference personalities make.'
Henry Kissinger

'From the sublime to the ridiculous is a single step.'
Napoleon Bonaparte